Yoga-Meditation Krishna-Patanjali Archives

Michael Beloved

Executive Editor: Bhakti Devi Beloved

Shiva Art / Yoga Sutras book cover: Sir Paul Castagna

Uddhava Gita Explained book cover: Terri Stokes

Brahma Yoga Bhagavad Gita book cover: Terri Stokes

Bhagavad Gita English book cover: Praful Kharsani

Other graphics: Michael Beloved

Managing Editors: Marcia Beloved and Dear Beloved

Correspondence: Michael Beloved
                          18311 NW 8th Street
                          Pembroke Pines, FL 33029
                          USA

Email: axisnexus@gmail.com

Online Archive: michaelbeloved.com

Copyright ©2013 --- Michael Beloved

ISBN: **9781489529503**

Table of Contents

Introduction

This is an information archive of the books authored by Michael Beloved on the subjects of yoga and meditation, reincarnation, astral projection, supernatural/spiritual perception, Krishna's and Patanjali's teachings.

Our intent is to give insight into Michael's writings.

Who are we?

His children: Dear Beloved, Bloom Beloved, Bhakti Devi Beloved and Draupadi Devi Beloved

Needless to say, we are impressed by the literary and informational output of our Dad. We think you will learn from each book you choose to read.

Let's begin!

Part 1
Series Descriptions

Michael Beloved began writing books on astral projection and meditation in 1969, before any of his children were born. His first book was produced in 1970 in the Philippines. At the time he found that he was explaining and re-explaining aspects of astral projection, reincarnation and meditation to interested people.

He hypothesized that it would be easier if he wrote a book. He could give copies to inquiring persons rather than spending hours explaining the same experiences to one person after another.

He got an 8½" X 14" lined yellow pad and began his first book. To his surprise, everything he had to say was written on 1½ sheets of this paper. He was disappointed. Writing books was not as easy as speaking. Mental completion of a book is not the same as the documented physical text.

He created four books which were never printed and which manuscripts are currently extinct. Those books were produced using carbon paper to make three copies from one type-sheet.

Some years after with the help of our mothers, Sharon Thornton and Marcia Beloved, he produced spiral bound books and booklets.

Later when the Print on Demand process became the norm, his dear friend, Sir Paul Castagna, suggested that he use that system to publish books. At first our Dad hesitated because he was unfamiliar with computers and never wanted to go main-stream. Sir Paul persisted and kept nudging him to do this. Eventually he relented and took to the task. Today, his publications are available through Amazon, Kobo and Kindle.

Bundling the Books

His books came to be categorized organically and were not written as a planned series.

Here is how we bundled them:

English Series:

Bhagavad Gita English
Anu Gita English
Uddhava Gita English
Markandeya Samasya English
Yoga Sutras English

Meditation Series:

Meditation Pictorial
Meditation Expertise

Explained Series:

Bhagavad Gita Explained
Uddhava Gita Explained
Anu Gita Explained

Commentary Series

Yoga Sutras of Patanjali
Meditation Expertise
Krishna Cosmic Body
Anu Gita Explained
Bhagavad Gita Explained
Kriya Yoga Bhagavad Gita
Brahma Yoga Bhagavad Gita
Uddhava Gita Explained

Specialty Series:

Spiritual Master
sex you!
Sleep Paralysis
Astral Projection

Unwrapping the Bundles

English Series

These are pocket-sized books of English translations of Sanskrit texts which relate to yoga, meditation and the ancient Indian way of approaching transcendence. The value of the Indian method is that the ancient yogis maxed out on the psyche. Theirs is, perhaps, more complete than any contribution from every other culture combined. There are five books in this category:

Bhagavad Gita English

Anu Gita English

Uddhava Gita English

Markandeya Samasya English

Yoga Sutras English

These are in twenty-first century English. Many Sanskrit words which were considered to be untranslatable into a Western language are rendered in modern English in an expressive and precise manner, due to the English language becoming the world's most frequent means of concept conveyance.

Three of these books are instructions from Krishna. In *Bhagavad Gita* and *Anu Gita*, the instructions were for Arjuna. And in the *Uddhava Gita*, Krishna gave instructions to Uddhava. *Bhagavad Gita* and Anu Gita are extracted from the *Mahabharata*. *Uddhava Gita* is extracted from the 11th Canto of the *Srimad Bhagavatam* (*Bhagavata Purana*).

Our suggestion is that you read *Bhagavad Gita English,* then *Anu Gita English,* then *Uddhava Gita English,* which is much more complicated and detailed.

Markandeya Samasya English may be tackled next. It is a revelation given by Krishna to the yogi Markandeya about the storage of the material cosmos when Brahma, a deity whose mind is the subtle existential support of the world, enters into slumber.

Markandeya was transferred from a supernatural ocean in which the physical universe was dissolved. He found himself trashing about in that cosmic sea. Then, he discovered an infant floating on a giant leaf, which grew from a cosmic tree.

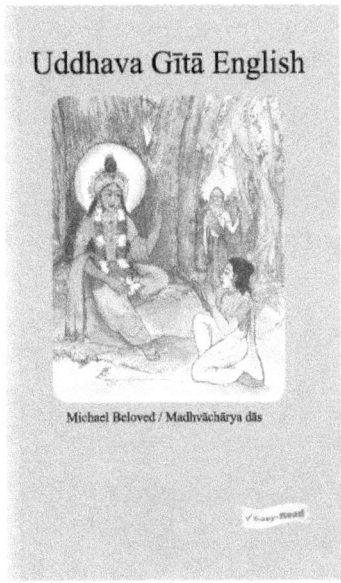 

The divine child spoke to Markandeya, explaining details of the dissolved creation. Markandeya was ingested into the mouth of that divine child. The yogi found himself in the stomach of the infant in the same world which was inundated by the cosmic sea.

Wandering about for millions of years, Markandeya saw the wonders of creation which he experienced before in the material world. Then when he was baffled and could not figure how the creation existed, he desired an interview with the infant. He was expelled through the mouth of the child's divine body.

This story is downright fascinating and is well worth the read!!

The final book in the English series is the *Yoga Sutras English*. Patanjali is accredited as the author of the Yoga Sutras which he produced in Sanskrit. This is the classic curriculum of yoga practice, the ashtanga or eight-part course for mastery of the mind. Due to his advanced meditation practice, our Dad was just as explicit in the English as Patanjali was in the Sanskrit.

If you are an advanced meditator, you will not regret reading the Yoga Sutras. If you are a novice and are curious about yoga, you will gain insight from it.

Meditation Series

There are two books in this series:

Meditation Pictorial

Meditation Expertise

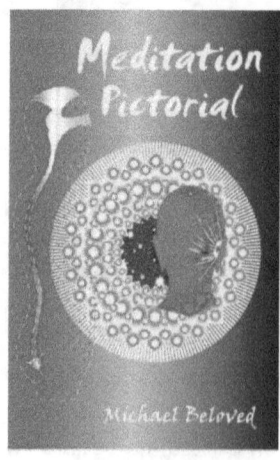

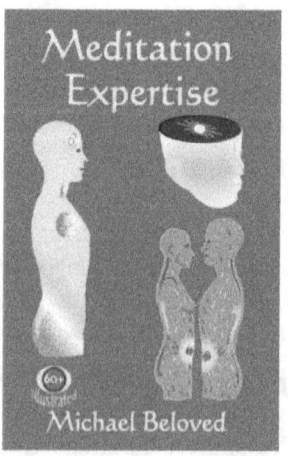

The specialty of these books is the mind diagrams which profusely illustrate what is written. The diagrams show exactly what you can do mentally to develop and sustain a meditation practice.

In the *Meditation Pictorial*, you are shown how to develop psychic insight, a feature without which meditation is reduced to imagination and visualization, without mystic experience.

In the *Meditation Expertise*, you are shown how to corral your practice to bring it in line with the classic syllabus of yoga which Patanjali lays out as the ashtanga yoga eight-staged procedure.

Both books are profusely illustrated with mind diagrams showing the components of psychic consciousness and the inner design of the subtle body.

Explained Series

There are three books in the Explained Series:

Bhagavad Gita Explained

Uddhava Gita Explained

Anu Gita Explained

These books are free of missionary intentions, cult tactics and philosophical distortion. Instead of using these books to add credence to a philosophy, meditation process, belief or plea for followers, the information is spread out so that you can look through this literature and freely take or leave anything as desired.

When Krishna stressed himself as the Supreme Being, that is stated. When He laid no claims for supremacy, none is awarded. You are free to form an independent opinion about the validity of the information and the credibility of Krishna.

There is contrast in the discourse with Arjuna in the Bhagavad Gita and the one with Uddhava in the Uddhava Gita. In fact these two books may appear to contradict each other. In the Bhagavad Gita, Krishna pressured Arjuna to complete social duties. In the Uddhava Gita, Krishna insisted that Uddhava should abandon the same.

The Anu Gita is not as popular as the Bhagavad Gita but it is the conclusion of that text. Anu means: "what follows". In this discourse, an anxious Arjuna requested that Krishna should repeat the Bhagavad Gita and again show His supernatural and divine forms.

However Krishna refused to do so and chastised Arjuna for being a disappointment in forgetting what was revealed. Krishna then cited a celestial yogi, a near-perfected being, who explained the process of transmigration in vivid detail.

Commentary Series

There are eight books with commentaries by the author:

Yoga Sutras of Patanjali

Meditation Expertise

Krishna Cosmic Body

Anu Gita Explained

Bhagavad Gita Explained

Kriya Yoga Bhagavad Gita

Brahma Yoga Bhagavad Gita

Uddhava Gita Explained

Bhagavad Gita Explained shows what was said in the Gita without religious overtones and sectarian biases.

Kriya Yoga Bhagavad Gita shows Krishna's instructions for mastery of kriya yoga.

Brahma Yoga Bhagavad Gita shows the instructions for proficiency in brahma yoga.

Uddhava Gita Explained details the instructions to Uddhava which are more advanced than the discussion with Arjuna.

Bhagavad Gita is an instruction for applying the expertise of yoga in the cultural field. This is why the process taught to Arjuna is called karma yoga which means karma + yoga or cultural activities managed with a yogic insight.

Uddhava Gita is an instruction for applying the expertise of yoga to attaining spiritual status. It explains jnana yoga and bhakti yoga in detail. Jnana yoga is using mystic skill for knowing the spiritual part of existence. Bhakti yoga is for developing affectionate relationships with divine beings.

Karma yoga is for negotiating the social concerns in the material world. It is inferior to bhakti yoga which concerns negotiating the social concerns in the spiritual world.

This world has a social environment and the spiritual world has one too.

Presently, Uddhava Gita is the most advanced and informative spiritual book on the planet. It verified that historically Krishna is the most advanced human being to ever have left written instructions on this planet. Even Patanjali Yoga Sutras which I translated and gave an application for in my book, *Meditation Expertise,* does not go as far.

Some information of the Yoga Sutras and the Uddhava Gita is identical but while the Yoga Sutras are concerned with the personal spiritual emancipation (kaivalyam) of the individual limited spirit, the Uddhava Gita goes further by explaining the situations in the spiritual universes.

Bhagavad Gita is from the Mahabharata which is the history of the Pandavas. Arjuna, the student of the Gita, is one of the Pandava brothers. He was in a social bind and did not know how to apply yoga expertise for a solution. Krishna gave him a crash-course on the battlefield on the application of yoga proficiency to cultural activities.

Uddhava Gita is from the Srimad Bhagavatam (Bhagavata Purana), which gives a history of the incarnations of Krishna. Uddhava was a relative of Krishna. He was concerned about the situation of the deaths of many relatives but Krishna diverted Uddhava attention to the practice of yoga for the purpose of successfully migrating to the spiritual environment.

The *Yoga Sutras of Patanjali* is divided into three parts:

- Translation into English with word-for-word meanings
- An approach in simple English based on the author's practice and integration of the method of the Sutras
- Verses in Sanskrit and English with Commentary

Meditation Expertise is another commentary of the Yoga Sutras with an application followed by analysis of each verse.

 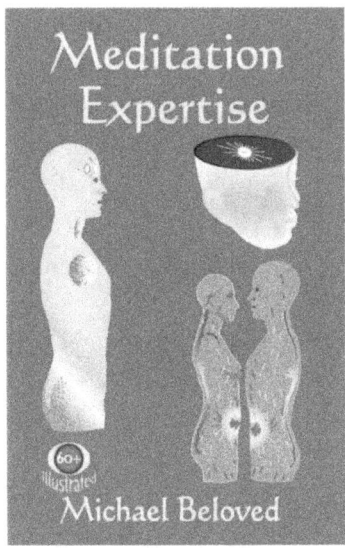

Krishna Cosmic Body is a translation and commentary of the Markandeya Samasya part of the Mahabharata, the description of Markandeya's supernatural experiences with Krishna, the divine boy.

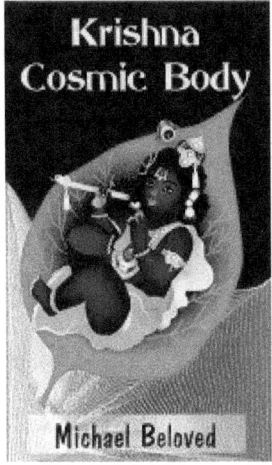 

Anu Gita Explained is a translation and commentary of the Anu Gita portion of the Mahabharata. This book is the ultimate book on how the consequences of our actions cause us to reach particular destinations in the hereafter. It explains how we are placed in the future history of the physical world.

Specialty Series

These books are based on Michael's personal experiences in meditation, yoga practice, reincarnation and guru relationship:

Spiritual Master

sex you!

Sleep Paralysis

Astral Projection

In *Spiritual Master,* Michael draws from experience with gurus or with their senior students. His contact with astral gurus is rated. He walks you through the avenue of gurus showing what you should do and what you should not do, so as to gain proficiency in whatever area of spirituality the guru has proficiency.

sex you! is a masterpiece about the adventures of an individual spirit's passage through the parents' psyches. The conversion of a departed soul into a sexual urge is described. The transit from the afterlife to residency in the emotions of the parents is detailed. This is about sex and you; learn about how much of you comprises the romantic energy of your would-be parents!

Sleep Paralysis clears misconceptions so that one can see what sleep paralysis is and what frightening astral experience occurs while the paralysis is being experienced. This disempowerment has great value in giving you confidence that you can and do exist even if you are unable to operate the physical body. The implication is that one can exist apart from and will survive the loss of the material body.

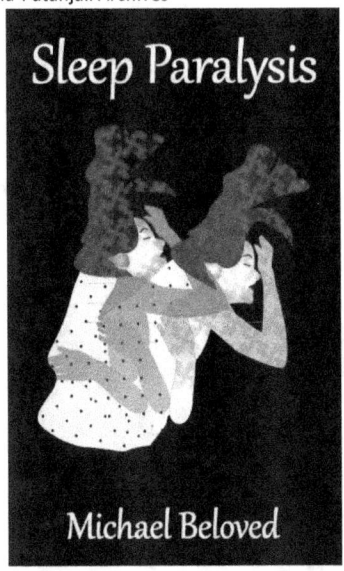

Astral Projection details experiences Michael had even in childhood, where he assumed incorrectly that everyone was astrally conversant. He discusses the life force psychic mechanism which operates the sleep-wake cycle of the physical form, and which budgets energy into the separated astral form which determines if the individual will have dream recall or no objective awareness during the projections. Astral travel happens on every occasion when the physical body sleeps. What is missing in awareness is the observer status while the astral body is separated.

Part 2
Book Descriptions,
including back cover text,
author's comments and reviews

sex you!

The story of your life before this life and hereafter.
The link between this and reincarnation.
Your ancestors as part of your sexual pleasure.
Has your great grandfather taken birth as your son?
Are you depriving your ancestor of an embryo
by using contraceptives or sexual protection?
Were you present at the sexual urge when your parents
were in the act of containing your present body?
This information gives insight into what you did
before you discovered yourself as a human body.

Publisher: Michael Beloved

Date: March 13, 2010

ISBN:

Print: 9780981933245

eBook: 9780981933276

LCCN: 2010901772

Page count: 260

Illustrations: 166

Size: 5 x 8 x 0.7 inches

Language: English

Category:

Body, Mind & Spirit, Reincarnation

Back Cover:

The story of your life before this life and hereafter.

The link between sex and reincarnation.

Your ancestors as part of your sexual pleasure.

Has your great grandfather taken birth as your son?

Are you depriving one of your ancestors of an embryo by using contraceptives or sexual protection?

Were you present as the sexual urge when your parents were in the act of conceiving your present body?

This information gives insight into what you were doing before you discovered yourself as a human being.

Description:

The mystery of sex and reincarnation is explained in detail, not in terms of religion or superstition but by psychic facts which any individual can observe, if he or she can shift focus to the psychic plane. Books like the Tibetan Book of the Dead (Bardo Thodol) and the Egyptian Book of the Dead (Papyrus of Ani), along with Bhagavad Gita, the reincarnation teaching of Buddha and other vital books, took humanity through a spiritual leap through time into the hereafter.

Perhaps none of these texts dealt with the incidences of sex and reincarnation head on, especially the link between you and the sexual act of your parents which produced your body. In this book you get the details in plain terms without mystery and religious impositions.

Reviews:

Vrettos Notaras -- "Billy" (Canada):

Thought provoking, perspective shifting literature on the interaction between the psychic and physical worlds! Readers familiar with the Upanishads and the Bhagavad Gita (unlike me) will probably recognize the theoretical foundation upon which the author rests his 40+ years of "minute observations". For me, this book provides insight and information that contradicts and undermines many of my theories on life. Fascinating, because it gives meaning to many astral experiences that I have had in the past. Burdensome, because the more you begin to read and reflect the more you know you need to learn. The delivery of the literature is extremely efficient and concise, which is something that I have never seen with books that try to deal with this complex subject matter. You will be crystal clear regarding the author's intent by the end of the book.... whether you agree, disagree, or choose to forget is up to you... but at least, now you know...

Surya das -- A Unique Contribution to the Path of Mystic Yoga

An exceptional book with the greatest insight into the explicit sexual dynamic of reincarnation. In addition, this most wonderful book by Michael Beloved offers extensive advice that will allow one to have a practical role in the process of the spirit soul's re-entry in material existence from the subtle world. The numerous diagrams ascertain that the manual is user friendly.

sex-you! does not leave a stone unturned and, is a unique and unparalleled contribution to anyone who takes advantage of its content.

Terri A. Stokes (Enchanted Rock, TX)

A brave little book for yoga/spirituality practitioners. Little known facts on dealing with the sexual urges are boldly discussed; ancestors coming through who are trying to exist again on this earth. One will learn quickly the facts about the "birds and bees", yoga style-reincarnation, how each of us enters into existence to live in these human bodies. Believe it or not, it is a fascinating and powerful book that gives the reader an unusual perspective on sexual passions. There are many questions. Still, I think that if a person is childless, our ancestors are honored by living everyday sharing one's inner Light with others and remembering that we are sacred because we walk between heaven and earth. Namaste

Neil Crenshaw, (McIntosh, Florida):

I must say that this book is a way-out book. It depicts sex as an act between a man and a woman mainly for spirits of the astral world (disembodied souls) to inhabit a woman's body and be born a human. The book is incredibly interesting but is not prefaced by anything that can substantiate this theory of reincarnation other than the author's claim that he got the information from the psychic world.

One must read this book with an open mind and simply enjoy the musings of the author as one would read an interesting book of fiction. How Michael spins the tale of souls "waiting in the wing" to be guided by a special deity is indeed intriguing to say the least. The idea that sexual urges and emotions of humans are created by those disembodied souls is truly original. The author covers how lust changes as we age, how drugs affect our ability to have sex, the role of the semen in the man and the egg in the woman and what happens to the disembodied souls during masturbation and homosexual acts.

There are many illustrations accompanying the author's discussions on masturbation, mystic sex, sexual intercourse and anatomy. Even if you know, or think you know, a lot about the conventional sexual habits of humans you will be educated in the mystic realm of human sexual behaviors. I would have to give this book five stars for originality, imagination, writing style and graphics and four stars for the entertainment value. There could be a section explaining how the author arrived at his ideas for this book. This would make it even more interesting.

Alfredo Delregato (Amazon customer review):

"sex you!" is at its core a yogic book, a mystic book derived from knowledge obtained through the power of yoga.

It cannot be an invention. Who can invent such a tale? Who could weave such an intricate interaction, not to mention such a displeasing one to those who place the value of sex on the altar of the god of pleasure?

For, aren't we told by medical authorities and "sex experts" that continuing making love beyond progeny with our partners and into old age is healthy for the body, prevents diseases, and other similar panacea? Wait, aren't these same medical authorities those who mostly promote a "balanced diet" when dealing with illnesses like cancer, which allow sugar, meat, and other polluting aliments? No surprise here.

Of the amazing details about the mystic intricacies of sex in all available particulars, including the responsibilities derived from engaging in it, and the primary role of ancestors, the other reviewers have already spoken, but that 2 important tenets of Hinduism (or Sanatana Dharma, the eternal religion), must be understood for a proper digestion of the material offered, should be stressed now, being these tenets: a) Reincarnation or transmigration of souls b) The existence of a hereafter where these disembodied spirits interact, push and shove, wait to re-enter the physical realm, this locations known as the astral worlds.

Finally, the most important value that this book has, is that it fills a void left by many a scripture of Hinduism and many commentaries on these scriptures, some by famous names, in that it explains the dynamics of reincarnation or rebirth in precise details. No other book in recent memory does that, please keep this in mind. Can these psychic processes be "proven"? Of course not, the scientists will cry! Of course not, we say, from a phenomenal point of view; but what about from a noumenal one? For we say that to ascribe lack of scientific approach to the science of yoga, from which these insights were derived, is the epitome of ignorance, for this knowledge comes from the best part of 40 years of psychic research where the author have alchemized his veracity into the crucible of his psyche and beyond. This is the same approach taken by the ancient Rishis of India. When the spermatozoon enters the egg, and life is "produced"...isn't it by magic? Let the scientists explain that.

Astral Projection

Astral projection is about self assurance of survival beyond the death of the physical system which a human being came to know as itself. It is the self-evidence that requires no other verification about the continuation and perpetuity of the psychological energies.

Every time the physical body sleeps, the psychological character separates from the physical form, and ventures into a subtle dimension, the astral world. It then returns into the physical casing and rises to continue its part in physical history. Supernatural nature conducts these operations, just as nature conducts the life and death of the physical body.

The evidence is subjective but it can be objectively verified by attentive dream awareness and observations of the shifts in consciousness from physical awareness to the stupor of sleep, and the existential transit from dreaming to physical waking.

Publisher: Michael Beloved

Date: August 27, 2012

ISBN:

Print: 9780984001378

eBook: 9780984001392

LCCN: 2012913750

Page Count: 140

Illustrations: 31

Size: 0.3 x 4.9 x 7.9 inches

Language: English

Category:

Religion and Spirituality

Back Cover:

Astral projection is about self-assurance of survival beyond the death of the physical system which a human being came to know as itself. It is the self-evidence that requires no other verification about the continuation and perpetuity of the psychological energies.

Every time the physical body sleeps, the psychological character separates from the physical form, and ventures into a subtle dimension, the astral world. It then returns into the physical casing and rises to continue its part in physical history. Supernatural nature conducts these operations, just as nature conducts the life and death of the physical body.

The evidence is subjective but it can be objectively verified by attentive dream awareness and observations of the shifts in consciousness from physical awareness to the stupor of sleep, and the existential transit from dreaming to physical waking.

Description:

---A paper on reincarnation, subtle body, astral projection, lucid dreaming, sleep paralysis, dimensional hoping, translation to paradise and transit to supernatural places.

Astral Projection is a natural psychic function which is not reliant on the conscious awareness of the person concerned. Day after day, usually once within every twenty-four hours, an individual spirit is displaced from its physical body normally while in a condition of stupor, unaware that it has separated. The individual then becomes conscious again as a physical body and gets busy to restart its physical activities. Astral projection is really the observation of that displaced psyche. This book divulges information on how to become conscious of this.

Author's Comment:

Astral Projection is the sure way to know that you are not just a material body, that you have a subtle form, a dream-form if you prefer to regard it as that. This form will survive the physical body.

Knowing how that form operates is even more important than knowing how the physical system exists. Take the time now to study that form so that when the physical body is no longer serviceable, when the time comes where you will no longer be able to identity with it as you, you can move on with ease into the astral dimensions.

Too much of a pre-occupation with the physical, results in fear of death of the physical body and in a feeling of anguish and deprivation when one is forced later on to live in the astral world permanently. This information would give you some insight into what the astral world is, how the astral body functions in it and what possibilities exist there as living situations.

Sleep Paralysis

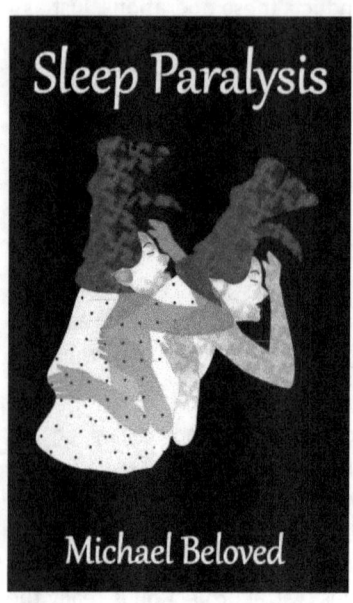

In simple terms, giving his experience of it since childhood, Michael dissects the psyche of the human being showing what controls sleep paralysis and how to decrease the incidences of it. No magic bullets! No, "You-can-control-everything" feel-good phrases!

Act to increase your limited control of existential states. Get hints of what you may do to increase positive experiences during dream and semi-conscious conditions.

There is a valuable hint in this paper about the realization of the self apart from the material body. Turn your sleep drama into a source of spiritual confidence. Use it to fathom your personality as a psychological reality existing apart from the physical body.

Publisher: Michael Beloved

Date: July 25, 2012

ISBN:

Print: 978-0984001361

e-Book: 9780984001385

LCCN: 2012913595

Page Count: 114

Illustrations: 25

Size: 8 x 5 x 0.3 inches

Language: English

Categories:

Religion and Spirituality

Back Cover:

In simple terms using my experiences since childhood, I dissect the psyche of the human being, showing what controls sleep paralysis and how to decrease the incidences of it.

No magic bullets! No, "You-can-control-everything" feel-good phrases!

Act to increase your limited control of existential states. Get hints of what you may do to increase positive experiences during dream and semi-conscious conditions.

There is a valuable hint in this paper about the realization of the self apart from the material body. Turn your sleep drama into a source of spiritual confidence. Use it to fathom your personality as a psychological reality existing apart from the physical body.

Description:

--- A short to-the-point paper on the psychic cause of sleep paralysis, how to manage it and decrease incidences.

The relationship between sleep paralysis and astral projection is explained. The methods of decreasing the incidences of sleep paralysis, increasing dream recall and being objectively conscious during astral projections is described. Most revealing of all, the author describes of his sleep paralysis states and what he did to contain these, get out of these and cause his psychic self to separate from and to fuse into the physical body without incidence.

Author's Comment:

One person's psychic experience is another person's concept only. Even so, such experience can be used as an orientation to other realities. The big problem with acquiring mystic insight is having a distrust of psychic states in which the observing self has little or no control. However that will not help in gaining the perception.

To that end, this book was written to give inexperienced persons some information about sleep paralysis of the physical body and the astral occurrences which happen during those phases.

Experienced persons can use this information for a comparison with their own observations during sleep paralysis. Spooky experiences which occur during sleep paralysis may be interpreted by the mind as being the cause of or as being linked to the paralysis. However in most cases, this is not true and the spooky experiences are coincidental.

In this book, I explained the causes of sleep paralysis and gave methods of dealing with it. I did this without downgrading nature's part in the experience.

Reviews:

Disconnects Between Astral and Physical Bodies -- by John Wilson

This is a primer on sleep paralysis. It's unique from other books on this matter because Michael Beloved links the sleep paralysis to a disconnect between the astral and physical bodies. He describes the `malfunction of sleep paralysis' as a valuable disconnect that allows us to achieve psyche-realization. We see our SELF as individual and apart from the body we inhabit. If the life force operated as normal all the time, we would have no objectivity on the self.

I would add to the book that one of the causes of sleep paralysis can also be a cutoff of blood supply to the limbs while asleep, which causes a disconnect when awakening. I've experienced sleep paralysis in a variety of conditions, and if my arm falls asleep due to sleeping on my shoulder awkwardly, I will often have a hard time awakening and when I finally awaken, I'll realize that my arm is fully asleep.

Final words...it's an easy read with pictures like many of his latest books. It's very straightforward and in plain language. Have fun reading it and perhaps you may look back on some of your dream experiences as a young child, and later on as an adult, in a different manner.

Thanks for the insight, Michael. I don't need to fear it anymore.

Brings Up Different Points of View -- Amazon customer review by Christoper D. Puksta

I am a religious person myself. My religion has played a big role in my life. With that said, I came at this book with a grain of salt and will still do so. The book offers religious like answers to some questions associated with sleep paralysis. Often these answers go against my religious convictions. However, I did appreciate how I was able to learn other facets of sleep paralysis that I would not have otherwise have heard. The religious part of this book wasn't really the problem for me, for like I said, knowing different views is very important and kinda entertaining. However, I wish the author cited his sources. He seems to say things that sound like they are just too much to come from one's own experience. Some citations and footnotes are needed for a better rating, so that someone like me, who respects what is written, but doesn't want to take everything to heart because it goes against his own convictions, can better understand where the author is coming from and then maybe in the end not be so scared to accept some more facts that the book states.

Spiritual Master

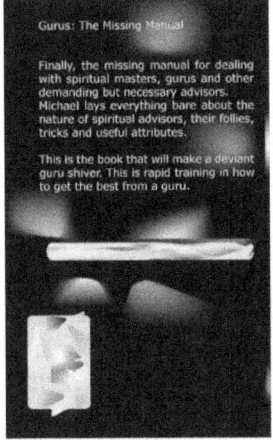

Publisher: Michael Beloved
Date: August 10, 2009
ISBN:

Print: 9780981933238

eBook: 9780981933269

LCCN: 2009904389

Page Count: 258
Illustrations: 6

Size: 5.25 x 8 x 0.7 inches

Language: English

Categories: Body, Mind, Spirit, Spirituality

Back Cover:

Gurus: The Missing Manual

---Finally, the missing manual for dealing with spiritual masters, gurus and other demanding but necessary advisors.

Michael lays everything bare about the nature of spiritual advisors, their follies, tricks and useful attributes.

This is the book that will make a deviant guru shiver. This is rapid training in how to get the best from a guru.

Description:

The origin, mission and necessity for gurus are elaborately described in this publication. The faults of gurus are shown. You are briefed in how to get techniques even from a deviant guru. The roles and leverage of disciples are shown. The various types of relationships between gurus and disciples are precisely discussed.

Author's Comment:

Practically every positive and negative aspect of having a guru is discussed in this book with recommendations of how to deal with gurus safely. A non-proficient guru can be useful despite his faults, but one must know how to side-step hassles and get to the business at hand, of gaining effective techniques from a spiritual master.

In some cases the spiritual master will be a complete fraud but one should not let that deter one from making spiritual progress in his association. "But why," one might ask, "should one stay with a fraudulent guru?" The answer is that if providence puts one in that position, one should honor destiny but one should do so without getting hurt by the unqualified spiritual master. This and similar topics are discussed in detail.

Reviews:

By Neil Crenshaw:

I just finished reading Michael Beloved's new book Spiritual Master. This book is very accessible and well-organized, but what makes it most engaging is the glimpse inside the world of people who profess to be specialists in helping others in spiritual matters. Michael answers the question as to whether spiritual masters are necessary to understand God and to be liberated from the material world.

What does it take to be liberated from the material world? Is a guru necessary for the transcendence? Michael attempts to answer these questions through his own past experiences with various gurus as well as being a guru himself. He outlines the pitfalls and the advantages of finding the proper guru to help guide one to a higher level.

The book is also very interesting to browse, thanks to the variety of topics relevant to each of us who are seekers, from the section about the different types of spiritual masters, to their limitations and misuse of power. Michael's passion for the topic and his experienced knowledge definitely help build a bridge to understanding the still-nascent and ever-evolving spiritual life of Western culture.

Krishna Cosmic Body

Imagine yourself as a human being the size of a virus or less. You enter into the body of a being who is the form of the universe. You tour that cosmic body knowing that you are inside the supernatural physiology of that transcendental personality.

A similar experience was related long ago by a yogi named Markandeya to Yudhishthira, a banished king in India. Markandeya identified Krishna who was present during the discourse as the Deity who is the form of the universe, the very same person whose cosmic body he entered long ago.

This is told in narrative form in the first ten chapters. It is given in its Sanskrit original, with transliterated English, word-for-word meaning and English translation. In the last two chapters. This is exciting. Is it science fiction, legend or experience of a master-mystic?

This was extracted from the Mahābhārata, that great literature which ancient India contributed to the library of the world.

Publisher: Michael Beloved

Date: January 26, 2012

ISBN:

Print: 9780984001323

eBook: 9780984001347

LCCN: 2012900736

Page Count: 274

Illustrations: 5

Size: 5" x 8" inches

Language: English

Category:

Body, Mind, Spirit, Meditation

Back Cover:

Imagine yourself as a human being the size of a virus or less. You enter into the body of a being who is the form of the universe. You tour that cosmic body knowing that you are inside the supernatural physiology of that transcendental personality.

A similar experience was related long ago by Yogi Markandeya to Yudhishthira, a banished king in India. Markandeya identified Krishna who was present during the discourse as the Deity who is the form of the universe, the same person whose cosmic body he entered long ago.

This is revealed in narrative form in the first ten chapters. It is given in its Sanskrit original, with transliterated English, word-for-word meanings and English translation in the last two chapters. This is exciting. Is it science fiction, legend or experience of a master mystic?

This was extracted from the Mahabharata, that great literature which ancient India contributed to the library of the world.

Description:

This is the amazing narrative of the Yogi Markandeya's survival of the cosmic dissolution of our universe and his re-instatement when it was created again. It tells of his entry into the divine infant Krishna, where he toured for millions of years through many existential locales as a tiny human being, like a bacteria in the body of a human.

Originally this tale was described in the Markandeya Samasya of the Mahabharata, an ancient Sanskrit literature from India. The value of this story is its presentation of the idea that our universe may be existing in the body of a deity, who is existing in the body of another deity who is the ultimate source.

At first Markandeya dealt with the cosmic dissolution but he was aware that his existential status relied on the energy in the mind of a deity named Brahma. When that deity fell asleep, all living beings inevitably slept in a blank mental state with no objectivity and with no distinct subjectivity either. Somehow Markandeya developed the ability to transcend this Brahma.

The yogi survived during Brahma's sleep but only to find himself in a violent ocean of cosmic water. He struggled for survival on that causal level of existence in which there were fearful astral aquatic creatures. Suddenly at a distance, he saw a gigantic banyan tree standing out of the water. He swam to it and saw an infant on a divine bedstead. The child had no concern for danger. Markandeya spoke to the infant and inquired of the kid's identity and location. He was drawn through the mouth of the infant into the infant's body where he spent millions of years. Then he was expelled and found himself in the cosmic sea again. The infant then explained the situation. He released the yogi to the original existence of the sub deity, Brahma.

This story was told by Vaishampaiana to King Janamejaya in the Mahabharata. It is worth read for all persons who do existential research.

Author's Comment:

Just in case you were wondering what it would be like if someone was the Supreme Being, how that person would accommodate planets, stars and creatures, then this is a book which can give the insight.

A great yogin named Markandeya experienced a divine boy into whose existence, this solar system is contained. Markandeya claimed to have lived in this divine being's body for trillions of years with the memory that he toured parts of the divine boy's supernatural body.

This discourse explains the situational position of God in reference to our existence and also in reference to beings who are supernaturally superior to us. One such being is named Brahma. Markandeya, even though he was jurisdictionally under Brahma's control, was empowered by the divine boy, to transcend Brahma's existence and to experience the extra-dimensional life which is outside Brahma's mental reach.

Living in the mind of someone else?

Being even less than a complete thought of the Supreme Being?

Delve into this story and get a glimpse!

Meditation Pictorial

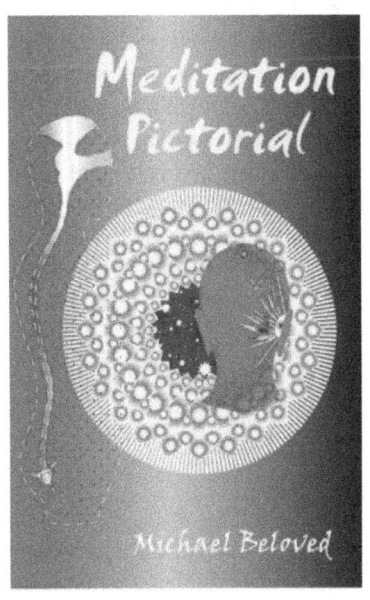
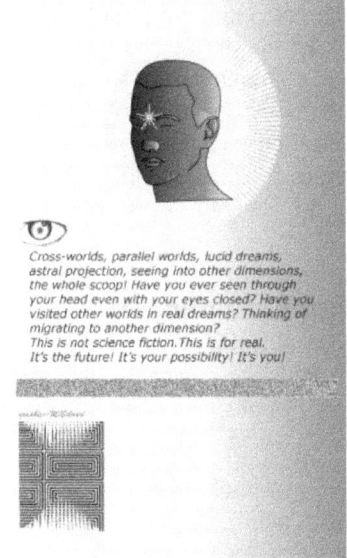

Publisher: Michael Beloved

Date: April 21, 2009

ISBN:

Print: 9780981933221

eBook: 9780981933290

LCCN: 2009902672

Page Count: 248

Illustrations: 180

Size: 9" x 6" x 0.7 inches

Language: English

Category:

Body, Mind, Spirit, Meditation

Back Cover:

Cross-worlds, parallel worlds, lucid dreams, astral projection, seeing into other dimensions, the whole scoop! Have you ever seen through your head even with your eyes closed? Have you visited other worlds in real dream experiences? Thinking of migrating to another dimension? Are you ready to clock out from the physical side?

Go to the other dimensions. Orient yourself by transitioning your psyche to a preferred cross-world before the physical body reaches its termination.

Though this is for real, it borders on science fiction. It's the future. It's you!

Description:

--- A detailed description of astral projection, lucid dreaming, cross world experience and the yogic and mystic methods which were used to see through the third eye. More than 150 illustrations show the opened third eye and the energized kundalini and other aspects of mystic practice. The subtle body is described in detail. Illustrations show how this body floats. Meditation techniques are discussed. Instructions are given for individual practice. This is a one-of-a-kind publication, produced by a kundalini yoga master, after 40 years of experience in samadhi trances and conscious astral projections.

Author's Comment:

This book was originally published in a small spiral booklet. It was the first in a series of such booklets. This publication however, consists of all those booklets in one volume.

This is essential for those who desire to experience the subtle and spiritual worlds, before departing the body. Basically speaking there are two kinds of spiritual aspirants, those who are careful to pursue spiritual experience during the life of the material body and those who do not care for that.

This book is helpful to those who want the experience now and do not want to wait until the death of the body to know for sure what is beyond this physical plane.

Believe it or not this book has over 150 diagrams showing the subtle body, the chakras, the mystic antics required in meditation and much more. This is a very essential book if you are interested in spiritual experience.

Reading Vedic literatures like Bhagavad Gita, which I translated and wrote commentaries for, is one thing. Experiencing the spiritual truths is another matter. The way you may experience the spiritual truths initially might not tally with what you read in the scriptures. But that initial stage is a clearing stage to prepare you for more clarity. This book shows much about what will happen in that clearing stage. This information could save you from much confusion and doubt and set you firmly on the spiritual path of self-purification.

Reviews:

By J.W. Wilson:

Meditation Pictorial came just a couple days after I ordered it and it took me a weekend to read the entire book. It's very interesting and relevant to people at all levels. Unlike some of Michael Beloved's other books, it's very easy to read for anyone and includes many anecdotal experiences gained by the author over 40 years of research in meditation. It easily contains over 100 pictures to illustrate key meditation techniques and references throughout the book.

As far as content, expect to learn a lot about the mind and body and also the interactions between our physical and subtle bodies. You will learn about dream states, how to open your third-eye and how to reverse energy flows within your body to achieve higher states of focus. The book spends a lot of time on tracking your thoughts and impulses and determining their true source. To add further credibility to his points, he aptly references the Bhagavad Gita on several occasions.

Many misconceptions about yoga, meditation, and its true purpose are addressed in this book. Faulty expectations are also pointed out. For example, at one point, he notes that "The impetus for liberation comes in an instant, but the actual process of being liberated takes time." Unfortunately most people, I included, want to get it overnight.

By Marcia Metusalem:

This is an interesting, conversational account of one yogi's mystic progression. The author gives many useful, illustrated, meditative techniques. He shares his own subtle experiences, describes the actual process of reincarnating, and emphasizes thought control and dream recall. This presentation sets the stage for meditation and opens a window to what may be experienced through deliberate, calculated, steady practice.

By D. Beloved:

Meditation Pictorial is an excellent read for anyone interested in yoga, meditation and an understanding of what is beyond the physical world. The author does a great job of conveying the complex path to mystic attainment in laymen's terms and provides clear diagrams on what may seem to be very subjective invisible points of focus to an untrained eye. The author provides concise directions on how to prepare one's body for life after death and the cleansing process required in order to reach the highest level of meditation. Overall I enjoyed this read and allowed the book to stretch my mind and see beyond just this physical materialistic life.

Other stand-out topics were on the benefits of isolation vs. social mixing and striking the right balance in both directions, as well as paying attention to the external influences from widespread music today. Ultimately meditation is about personal attention applied to the psychic side.

You will change after reading this book and parts of it will make you uncomfortable as you realize the faults of your own human nature. Ironically, it ends without a clear direction for the reader, much like meditation itself!

By Sara Smith:

The book came in the mail the day after a friend ordered it for me. I understand meditation on a basic level and was able to understand much of the book. There were areas of the book that were written for someone who is practicing meditation on a more advanced level. These sections gave me great indications of what I could achieve if I worked hard. The pictures were plentiful and made some descriptions easier to understand for me as I am a visual learner.

One can set up better expectations for what they will derive from meditation and how long it will take to get expected results after reading this book. So if you're interested in your psychic side and how your physical body and 'subtle body' are related and how you can focus and change your thoughts and desires, this is the book for you. In this book you can learn about controlling your thoughts and recalling dreams you have.

The author uses his subtle experiences to bring reality to what you will read. It describes well the world that exists outside of the physical world that we can readily see. Reincarnation and life after death are also covered in this quick read. Ultimately no one can advance your meditation for you - it's a self-directed journey.

By Neil Crenshaw:

This book deals with the supernatural, mythical as well as the practical side of meditation. Michael Beloved's book is not for the beginner for it delves deeply into the philosophical side of death, life and the hereafter and how they relate to meditation. This is not a book of simple meditation exercises, as many books on the subject are. Meditation Pictorial is filled with new concepts and ideas that are accompanied by excellent line drawings and illustrations. Some of the chapters seem disorganized with parts scattered here and there. But, the book presents a practical and honest approach to Michael's own experiences with life and meditation. One story describes the author's personal experience of a visit to Hell. He lays down instructions on what a person can do in this lifetime to prepare for death and for the next life successfully. Michael also deals with the life force that dwells within us all and ways to control that force through breathing techniques and observations. This book would be very good for those who are interested in exploring deeper into their meditation practice.

By A Bravo (Amazon customer review):

THIS IS PRETTY GOOD IF YOU EVER NEED TO ELABORATE ON ANY MEDITATION JUST PICK UP THE BOOK AND CHECK IT OUT ALWAYS SOMETHING NEW TO LEARN HEAR. IM GLAD IT HAS COMPUTER GENERATED PICS NOT TOO MANY MEDITATION BOOKS HAVE THEM.

By Richard Kiskiel (Amazon customer review):

I have read meditation books too numerous to mention, since the 70's. What I find different and most useful about Meditation Pictorial are the pictures which show images of what you will come across in your mind. Without a teacher you will not understand that some of the images you see are not made up by your mind and in fact are major sign posts on the road to spiritual progress. A road map, with sign posts that eliminate it being the Twilight Zone but yet take you to the mystical connections of the universe and how it relates to you personally. Without this book I would not have been as inspired as I am, and I probably would not have had the experience of traveling through a Black Hole and entering the "Cave of Brahma" or "House of God".

You can spend endless amounts of time in your head with your thought processes, and not knowing what to do with them and how to decipher their value. So for me this book has been the equivalent of having a teacher when I did not have one. I have had teachers in the past, but to be honest the amount of detailed information revealed in this book about the spiritual path is priceless. The book might not be for beginners, but then again seeing the pictures would probably be inspirational to anyone because they ring true in your mind when you see them and then you want to achieve that state, and you know it is achievable.

By Moomin -- Using Your Third Eye (Amazon customer review):

Meditation Pictorial is a rich, practical workbook with step-by-step instructions for advanced meditation. An intensely spiritual read, you will learn about esoteric interpretations of lucid dreams, astral projection and other dimensions. If you are looking for new interpretations of awareness beyond the body, Meditation Pictorial may have the answers you seek.

Meditation Expertise

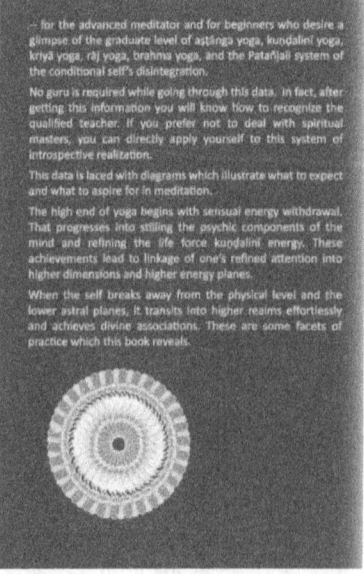

Publisher: Michael Beloved

Date: September 13, 2010

ISBN:

Print: 9780981933252

E-Book: 9780983381723

LCCN: 2010907496

Page Count: 284

Illustrations: 66

Size: 6 x 9 x 0.7 inches

Language: English

Category:

Body, Mind, Spirit, Meditation

Back cover:

-- For the advanced meditator and for beginners who desire a glimpse of the graduate level of ashtanga yoga, kundalini yoga, kriya yoga, raj yoga, brahma yoga, and the Patanjali system of the conditional self's disintegration.

No guru is required while going through this data. You can have it all to yourself, free of the harassments of an authority. In fact, after getting this information you will know how to recognize the qualified teacher. If you prefer not to deal with spiritual masters, you can directly apply yourself to this system of introspective realization.

This data is laced with diagrams which illustrate what to expect and what to aspire for in meditation.

The high end of yoga begins with sensual energy withdrawal. That progresses into stilling the psychic components of the mind and refining the life force kundalini energy. These achievements lead to linkage of one's refined attention into higher dimensions and higher energy planes.

When the self breaks away from this level of existence, it transits into higher realms effortlessly. It achieves divine associations. These are the facets of practice which this book reveals.

Description:

This is the translation, analysis, application and related diagrams for Patanjali's Yoga Sutras, the complete syllabus for yoga. This information about the techniques of advanced yoga is open to all, but it is of special interest to persons who meditated for years either in this or in a past life, and who now want to get to the culmination of yogic mysticism.

If there ever was a post graduate study and application of yoga, then Patanjali's Sutras are it. They map the path, show the way and reveal the elevated stages which are hard to reach even for those who mastered astral projection and third eye perception.

Chapter 1 gives the description and layout of samadhi transcendence accomplishment. Chapter 2 explains practice accomplishment. Chapter 3 shows the glory which may be attained by a persistent yogi. Chapter 4, the last, tells the yogi how to make the segregation accomplishment where the core-self is disconnected from its perception equipment and realizes itself as itself.

In the last chapter, there is an explanation of how to safely unify again with the perception equipment after the core-self is isolated from these. At the time of publication, there is no other media that goes into so much detail about advanced yoga practice.

Author's Comment:

This is the graduate study of the process of yoga as described by Patanjali. You can understand much even if you are not advanced but the essence of this would be accomplished by subtle techniques. I took great care in this translation and commentary and added an application to each verse. There are diagrams throughout the text.

Patanjali asked us to stop the ordinary operational procedures of the mind. To do this requires detailed observation of the maneuvers of the various parts of mind. With an understanding of the layout of consciousness as given by Patanjali, one can distinguish the various psychic organs and learn how to curtail their mundane involvements.

The accomplishment is to upgrade the psychic organs and to peer into higher dimensions. At first one has to sort the organs, determine their destructive operations and curtail those. Then one has to segregate the core-self from the organs so as to disempower them. That mystic action restores the self's integrity. One must also assume a set of highly energized psychic organs.

Reviews:

Very Easy Reading for a Difficult Concept -- by Dear Beloved

This is the full course of yoga explained concisely in the first thirty pages and fully expounded in the next 200 or so pages. I initially found myself closing my eyes and absorbing the information while reading it. There are tons of clear graphics that flow with the text.

It's very easy reading for a concept that's historically difficult to comprehend.

Reading this, I came away with a few conclusions. You don't have to be anyone special to do yoga or to have the powers that come with yoga. It's inherent in all of us. The same mental tool that we use impulsively or intentionally for imagination gives us the window into the supernatural world.

The sound 'Om' is not a mysterious mantra with secret powers. It's a physical effect on the brain from the reverberation of sound inside the skull and it provides an automatic bridge to the state of higher awareness.

This book takes a step forward by providing application at every step throughout. If you are unsatisfied with the rat race of survival - like me, or if you suffer from mood swings and instability - like others, you need to seriously consider taking up meditation and this would probably be the only book you'd ever have to read.

Past presumptions about yoga and what works and what doesn't, are crumbling in the face of revealing books like this one. Best wishes in your journey to open up the sky of consciousness.

Bhagavad Gita English

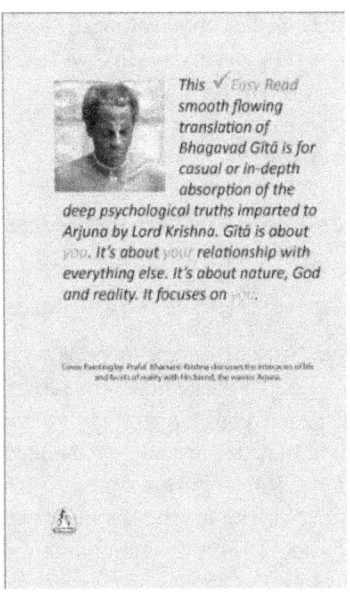

This ✓ Easy Read smooth flowing translation of Bhagavad Gītā is for casual or in-depth absorption of the deep psychological truths imparted to Arjuna by Lord Krishna. Gītā is about you. It's about your relationship with everything else. It's about nature, God and reality. It focuses on ...

Publisher: Michael Beloved

Date: November 14, 2008

ISBN:

Print: 9780979391637

eBook: 9780979391675

LCCN: 2008906310

Page Count: 176

Illustrations: 2

Size: 6.8 x 4.2 x 0.6 inches

Language: English

Category:

Religion and Spirituality

Description / Back Cover:

This easy-read smooth flowing translation of Bhagavad Gita is for casual or in-depth absorption of the deep psychological truths imparted to Arjuna by Lord Krishna. Gita is about you. It's about your relationship with everything else. It's about Nature, God and reality. It focuses on you.

Author's Comment:

This is just English. This is good for reading through the Bhagavad Gita to become familiar with the trend of the conversation between Lord Krishna and Arjuna.

This is pocket size, making it easy to carry in clothing or handbag.

Bhagavad Gita may seem strange but if one reads through it again and again, one begins to follow the conversation and acquire methods of improvement for spiritual life.

Reviews:

An easy read -- by Bernard Ajodhya:

This little Bhagavad Gita book is a sure must have. Why? because as the book cover says ... it's an easy read.

I have been carrying this book with me almost every day that I go to and from work. It easily fits in my jacket pocket and I read when on the train or bus. When you concentrate on the verses you can pretty much get the feeling that this discourse is being spoken right at that moment as you are reading. The language is easy to follow and the reading is like picking up a story book, but for those who are students of Gita, this is not like any other story book. There is also a large index, which is very handy when you just want to know about a particular word or topic.

To sum up, I have become found of this little book. It has made me more interested in wanting to read this text more and to be better familiarize with this discussion between the Person Krishna and His friend Arjuna. The author has done a very good job in presenting the Gita to those who prefer an easy read, but still desire an unbiased and honest interpretation.

Very good primer and reference -- by Jason Smith:

This translation of the ancient Bhagavad Gita is very straightforward and easy to use and reference. Complete with an index, I had no problem referring to any portion of the book. It's very small size was convenient as well.

As far as the content, the Bhagavad Gita is a timeless philosophical discourse that is both insightful and infinite in its wisdom. I highly recommend ordering this book and studying it, much like Sun Tzu--The Art of War. The book could perhaps have included some introductory discussion on the overall background of the Battle of Kurukshetra and the context of the time; however, this can be found in other places online if you aren't already familiar with the story.

Overall, a great read and a constant reference tool for how to live your life and make decisions.

Very accurate -- by Dear Beloved:

Compact, pocket-sized translation that was easy to read and understand and very accurate. I highly recommend this along with other classical philosophical texts like "The Art of War".

Does not oversimplify -- by Marcia Metusalem:

In the Bhagavad Gita, Krishna presents himself as the Supreme Person (God). He explains how human beings get psychologically stuck in material existence and gives a detailed process on how to become spiritually situated and at the same time be involved in cultural activity. Some of the concepts are mind bending; some must be taken in context of the ancient world. Any person who wants to go beyond organized, faith-based religion, will be drawn to and challenged by the Gita. This translation is written in modern English. It is precise but does not oversimplify or distort anything.

Great, by Psbra -- (Amazon customer review):

I've read other Mahabharatas and I can assure this version is a great obra. It's easy to assimilate and comfortable to read. Even my wife, who is Christian, is loving the Hindu story.

Your pocket Gita, by Bhakti M -- (Amazon customer review):

Great small copy of the Gita to carry with you everywhere; easy to read, to the point, and easy to search specific topics with the index. Read it on your lunch break, while traveling, or on your couch at home...gain a better understanding of the Bhagavad Gita! Another bonus is that the price is right!!

I gave this to my boyfriend -- by The Purrrr, MD, (Amazon customer review):

Since he's of Indian descent, he's read this twice & his older brother said he should read it 3 times. This has truly changed his outlook on life & his relationships... all for the better. I cannot wait till he's finished his 3rd reading so that I can read it.

-- by Raku Rudy (Amazon customer review):

This the second version of the Gita that I've read, and since I have it on my Kindle and phone, it is easy to read and reference. I like it. Aloha, Rudy.

A classic -- by Heather "Houndog" (Amazon customer review):

An easier version of the classic than most and is a little more understandable than other versions. Interesting concepts and theology.

Easy to read by Benjamin Thompson (Amazon customer review):

I have not read any other translation, but this one seemed pretty easy to read. Understanding it is a little harder!

Old-fashioned yet poetic, and a good value -- by N. Coppedge "Eucaleh Terrapin", (Amazon customer review):

I picked up this book in a used bookstore.

This is better than some of the other translations of the Gita, and I was surprised at how short it was. I read most of the book in an afternoon.

Although most readers are apt to find the index worthless, most of the features are un-obstreperous or impressive.

The scene in which Krishna manifests himself is especially impressive; it is difficult to see how it could be written a different way in English.

I believe unlike some other editions of the Gita, the book is divided into clearly separated Chapters, such as "Spiritual Teaching" and "Social Conduct".

I found these Chapter headings especially helpful in understanding the organization of the text.

Objective translation! -- By Krishna Prabhakar (Amazon customer review):

This is an objective translation with non-missionary and non-preaching style. Although the translation, sometimes, falls short of its objective as the author has gone for verbatim instead of the substance. But Sanskrit being an ancient language and the subject being Philosophical, such shortcomings are acceptable and part of the genre. But the prime objective of the book is to present The Bhagwad Gita in a simple and lucid manner and the author succeeds in that.

Good translation -- by Vaibhav Shrimali (Amazon customer review):

A good book for a non-Hindu to get to know the timeless words of the omniscient Krishna. I was happy to see that there were very few opinions from the author. It was more of translation.

Excellent Book of Historical Significance -- by Julian Harper (Amazon customer review):

I have read this epic many years ago and was very happy to get it again in electronic form. The book is very long so this format makes it very easy to carry about. I would recommend it for anyone interested in classic literature.

Anu Gita English

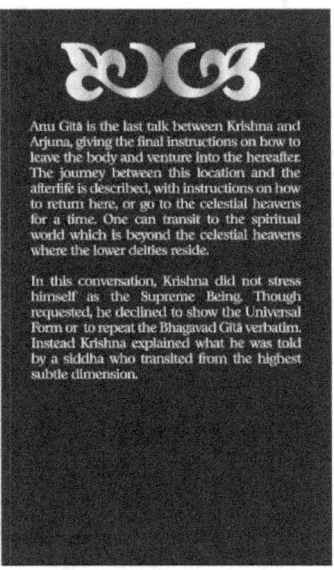

Anu Gitā is the last talk between Krishna and Arjuna, giving the final instructions on how to leave the body and venture into the hereafter. The journey between this location and the afterlife is described, with instructions on how to return here, or go to the celestial heavens for a time. One can transit to the spiritual world which is beyond the celestial heavens where the lower deities reside.

In this conversation, Krishna did not stress himself as the Supreme Being. Though requested, he declined to show the Universal Form or to repeat the Bhagavad Gītā verbatim. Instead Krishna explained what he was told by a siddha who transited from the highest subtle dimension.

Publisher: Michael Beloved   **Page Count:** 100

Date: August 31, 2011   **Illustrations:** 33

ISBN: **Size:** 4.25" x 6.88" (inches)

Print: 978-0983381785   **Language:** English

eBook: 9780984001309   **Category:**

LCCN: 2011914435   Body, Mind, Spirit, Reincarnation

Back Cover:

Anu Gita is the last talk between Krishna and Arjuna, giving the final instructions on how to leave the body and venture into the hereafter. The journey between this location and the afterlife is described, with instructions on how to return here, or go to the celestial heavens for a time.

One can go the spiritual world which is beyond the celestial heavens where the lower deities reside. In this conversation, Krishna did not stress himself as the Supreme Being. Though requested, he declined to show the Universal Form or to repeat the Bhagavad Gita verbatim. Instead Krishna explained what he was told by a siddha who transited from the highest subtle dimension.

Description:

Anu Gita is intense. It is Krishna's action thriller. Unlike the Bhagavad Gita where He explained many topics which were part of the course of the application of yoga proficiency to social involvement, the Anu Gita begins with an inquiry into the nature of the individual being and its transmigration between the physical world and the astral existence.

There is no drifting away from the topic. Krishna does not stress his divinity and supremacy as he did in the Bhagavad Gita. He simply quoted a discourse which occurred between a perfected siddha and Kashyapa. This discourse was told to Krishna by a yogi who came down from the highest celestial world.

Author's Comment:

This is concise, direct and point-blank information about what happens after death. Nature's mechanical and yet time-regulated lay out of circumstances can be perceived directly through spiritual perception. In the meantime those of us who do not have the mystic view, may learn a trick or two from this discourse. It is the most graphic description about the workings of reincarnation to be expounded yet.

Reviews:

Distilled and Raw Knowledge -- John Wilson, (Amazon customer review):

Anu Gita is an ancient and once-secret text in Sanskrit for which there are literally no recent or modern translations. This knowledge has been suppressed for decades and continues to be suppressed as many chase the illusory goal of happiness without ever reaching it. The path of astral projection, the psyche, the hereafter, the means of spirits entering and leaving this earthly realm and other related subjects are explained logically and concisely in an astonishing way.

If you are seeking, then THIS TRANSLATION IS AN EXCELLENT PLACE TO BOTH START AND FINISH, containing knowledge for the beginner and the advanced. The last translation in the book says, "This is all that is to be said. There is nothing beyond this. [...] one who practices proficiently and consistently for six months accomplishes this." And if you are really intrigued, then go for the Anu Gita Explained which has both analysis and application in addition to the translation.

Markandeya Samasya English

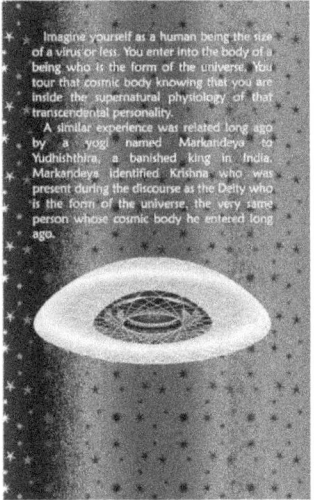

Publisher: Michael Beloved

Date: January 26, 2012

ISBN:

Print: 9780984001330

eBook: 780984001354

LCCN: 2012900737

Page Count: 84

Illustrations: 5

Size: 4.25" x 6.88" (inches)

Language: English

Category:

Body, Mind, Spirit, Meditation

Back Cover:

Imagine yourself as a human being the size of a virus or less. You enter into the body of a being whose form is the universe. You tour that cosmic body knowing that you are inside the supernatural physiology of that transcendental personality.

A similar experience was related long ago by a yogi named Markandeya to Yudhishthira, a banished king in India. Markandeya identified Krishna who was present during the discourse as the Deity who is the form of the universe, the very same person whose cosmic body he entered long ago.

Description:

This is the English translation of the Markandeya Samasya portion of the Mahabharata. This is in fluent English with no commentary. This same translation with the original Sanskrit and with a narrative explanation is published under the title of *Krishna Cosmic Body*.

This is the amazing narrative of the Yogi Markandeya's survival of the cosmic dissolution of our universe and his re-instatement when it was created again. It tells of his entry into the divine infant Krishna, where he toured for millions of years through many existential locales as a tiny human being, like a bacteria in the body of a human.

Originally this tale was described in the Markandeya Samasya of the Mahabharata, an ancient Sanskrit literature from India. The value of this story is its presentation of the idea that our universe may exist in the body of a deity, who exists in the body of another deity who is the ultimate source.

At first Markandeya deals with the cosmic dissolution but he is aware that his existential status relies on the energy in the mind of a deity named Brahma. When that deity fell asleep, all living beings inevitably slept in a blank mental state with no objectivity and with no distinct subjectivity either. Somehow Markandeya developed the ability to transcend this Brahma.

The yogi survived during Brahma's sleep but only to find himself in a turbulent ocean of cosmic water. He struggled for survival on that causal level of existence in which there were fearful astral aquatic creatures. Suddenly at a distance, he saw a gigantic banyan tree standing out of the water. He swam to it and saw an infant on a divine bedstead. The child had no concern for the dangers. Markandeya spoke to the infant and inquired of the kid's identity and location. He was drawn through the mouth of the infant into the infant's body where he spent millions of years. Then he was expelled and found himself in the cosmic sea again. The infant then explained the situation. He released the yogi to the original existence of the sub deity, Brahma.

This story was told by Vaishampaiana to King Janamejaya in the Mahabharata. It is worth the read for anyone who does existential research.

Author's Comments

This book was commissioned by a deceased great yogi. That person was known as Rishi Singh Gherwal in his last physical body. I did not meet Rishi on the physical level, but I heard of him from my first yoga teacher who was Arthur Beverford.

Rishi met me in the astral world asked me to do this translation of Markandeya's experience of the transcendental self of Krishna. This is the divine infant Krishna who floats on a leaf in a cosmic sea.

The commentary to this, with word for word meanings of the original Sanskrit text, is published under the title of *Krishna Cosmic Body*.

Markandeya experienced survival of cosmic destruction. He met the divine infant Krishna who explained how these worlds are created, maintained, and then demolished again.

Reviews:

An Existential Puzzle Revealed -- by John Wilson

This book is a small and easy read...got it in paperback and finished in a couple hours. It is a direct translation of a key portion of the *Mahabharata*.

I was reminded of the wayward bankers when reading of how a righteous lifestyle becomes replaced by dishonesty and fraudulent ways. Those who are honest become the bottom of the society and hold the least amount of wealth. But then this is shaken off by intense solar flares and fires and massive destruction, after which an era of renewal begins. I was particularly intrigued by the mention of seven blazing suns that evaporate all waters of oceans and rivers. Sounds like the end of a world and beginning of a new one.

Yoga Sutras English

This book is for beginner, intermediate and advanced yogis with special emphasis on what Patañjali had to say about yoga. The author had no intention of using these sutras to validate any meditation scheme.

There is no verse in the Sutras which describe yoga as being union or as being just based on the Sanskrit root word yuj. For that matter Patañjali defined yoga as having eight distinct and clearly definable parts.

If you practice you could estimate your position and progress by matching your experiences to the layout given by Patañjali. If you are just curious, you will be informed of the methods used in his time.

Publisher: Michael Beloved

Date: March 2011

ISBN:

Print: 9780983381709

eBook: 9780983381716

LCCN: 2011904133

Page Count: 122

Illustrations: 52

Size: 6.88 x 4.25 x 0.3 inches

Language: English

Category:

Body, Mind, Spirit, Meditation

Back Cover:

This book targets beginner, intermediate and advanced yogis with special emphasis on what Patañjali had to say about yoga. The author had no intention of using these Sutras to validate any meditation scheme.

There is no verse in the Sūtras which describes yoga as being union or as being just based on the Sanskrit root word yuj. For that matter Patañjali defined yoga as having eight distinct and clearly definable parts.

If you practice, you could estimate your position and progress by matching your experiences to the layout given by Patañjali. If you are just curious, you will be informed of the methods used in the time of Patanjali.

Description:

This is a detailed and very attentive translation of the Yoga Sutras of Patanjali. This is not for supporting any philosophy or legitimatizing ideas of oneness (advaita). It is not for using Patanjali to give validity to a concept of enlightenment or liberation. Patanjali's in-depth exploratory diagram of the human psyche is clear to see in this compressed thesis.

Reviews:

A Tiny Book with a Lot of Pics -- by John Wilson

I got this book as soon as it was released as a gift from the author. It's basically a simple translation of the classic Yoga Sutras texts. What he's done is put a lot of pictures in with the ancient yoga lessons. There are tons of pictures which I identified with a lot more than the text. I'm very visual and I found the pictures to be much easier to understand than the verses which you need to read a couple times to turn it over in your mind. I found that my default mode of operation in my mind is in the analytical orb that sits in front of the self. Most of the time I can't even reach the self because my analytical mind is working overtime. His best book yet and it can be read in a day or two if you go easy.

Uddhava Gita English

Publisher: Michael Beloved

Date: April 4, 2009

ISBN:

Print: 9780981933207

eBook: 9780981933283

LCCN: 2008911847

Page Count: 280

Illustrations: 3

Size: 4.25 x 6.88 x 0.7 inches

Language: English

Category: Religion Spirituality

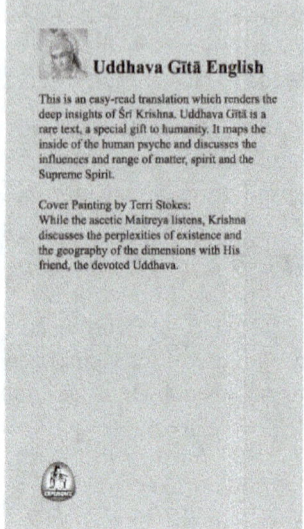

Back Cover:

Cover Painting by Terri Stokes: Krishna discusses the intricacies of life and facets of reality with His devotee Uddhava, while Maitreya, an ascetic, looks on.

Description:

This is an easy-read translation which renders the deep insights of Śrī Krishna. Uddhava Gītā is a rare text, a special gift to humanity. It maps the inside of the human psyche and discusses the influences and range of matter, spirit and the Supreme Spirit.

Author's Comment:

This is the English translation only. This is a handy pocket size edition, which could be carried in a man's pocket or woman's handbag. Take this along when you ride a bus or will be somewhere with spare time. Get to know what Lord Krishna told Uddhava which was not mentioned or recommended to Arjuna in Bhagavad Gita.

The commentary was published as *Uddhava Gita Explained*. Keep the commentary at home. It is a large book of some 740 pages. While reading this pocket volume, note topics of interest and read further in the commentary, when you have the time to do so.

Reviews:

Advanced Psychology, Human Nature and Inner Powers -- John Wilson

This is an entertaining and interesting read that covers advanced psychology, human nature and inner powers. It even speaks about the subtle hole at the head through which a spirit should depart at death, something that was a central piece of the Dan Brown novel "The Lost Symbol". It's a direct translation with very clear words and very potent information. Anyone interested in achieving a higher state of consciousness, clearing the cloudy confusion of materialism, or just learning ancient secrets that never change with time, should definitely read this...and not just once, but two or three times for deeper meanings.

Bhagavad Gita Revealed

Publisher: Michael Beloved

Date: November 1, 2008

ISBN:

Print: 9780979391620

eBook: 9780983381730

LCCN: 2008906318

Page Count: 310

Illustrations: 3

Size: 6 x 9 x 0.7 inches

Language: English

Category: Religion / Spirituality

Back Cover:

There are hundreds of translations of Bhagavad-Gītā. These fall into two general groupings, as those with missionary intentions and those of non-religious interest. This translation is not for promoting missionary work but it is not strictly speaking, devoid of religious interest. In so far as the Bhagavad-Gītā itself considers religion, this translation does the same.

This edition only shows what Śrī Krishna said and offers that in free style, leaving the reader to form independent conclusions. This is suited to those who want to view the Gītā without having missionaries, philosophers and historians exerting their influence.

Description:

--- An insightful, easy-read, word-for-word, non-sectarian translation with detailed indexes.

Author's Comment:

This volume has the Sanskrit (Devanagari) text, with word-for-word meanings in English. This has no commentary. This book is for you if you desire to peruse the Sanskrit carefully.

To sort between what Krishna said and what other religious authorities claim that He said, one has to check the Sanskrit. To see why the claims imposed by religious leaders on the Gita usually fail to manifest, one has to double check the Sanskrit text. If you are really serious about the Gita, take time to check the Sanskrit carefully. Sanskrit, unlike modern languages like English, has a set number of root words. This language is for all practical purposes static because it is no longer in general usage on this planet. That makes it an easy language to grasp, if one is patient enough to study it.

Reviews:

A Commentary That Leaves No Stone Uncovered -- by Jason Smith:

After reading this commentary, my life outlook vastly matured and quality of my actions increased. The Bhagavad Gita is one of those profound philosophical discourses that stands the infallible test of time. I actually ordered the author's original translation (Bhagavad Gita English), and then soon after I ordered this book to better understand the concepts.

Bhagavad Gita Explained

Publisher: Michael Beloved

Date: March 6, 2009

ISBN:

Print: 9780979391606

E-Book: 9780983381747

LCCN: 2008907393

Page Count: 596

Illustrations: 14

Trim Size: 7" x 10" (inches)

Language: English

Category:

Body, Mind, Spirituality

Back Cover:

As a philosophical treatise and a religious canon, Bhagavad-Gītā endured the test of time. With the prevalence of literacy, many hundreds of published and unpublished translations and commentaries abound. People find solace in the philosophy of Gītā and existential security in the promises given by Sri Krishna.

This exceptional translation and commentary opens an avenue to Krishna's explanations about the mysteries of material existence, the individual self and the Supreme Being. It answers many questions, some of which are:

Who are we? What is our purpose? Is there an eternal self? Is this physical world the one and only dimension?

Description:

As a philosophical treatise and a religious canon, Bhagavad-Gita stood the test of time. With the prevalence of literacy, many hundreds of published and unpublished translations and commentaries abound. People find solace in the philosophy of Gita and existential security in the promises given by Sri Krishna. Gita was abused and is still subjected to harassment by philosophers and preachers who find it necessary to use it to support their doctrines and claims.

This translation shows what Sri Krishna explained to Arjuna in terms of their cultural situation; at least in so far as the Mahabharata described.

This translation stands apart from others by its lack of exploitation of the Gita for missionary or philosophical purposes. Once you begin reading this, you may be reluctant to put it down. This really can put you in touch with Lord Krishna and with Arjuna, the initially discouraged but later courageous and enlightened warrior.

Author's Comment:

Originally published by Asian Printery in India, as *Bhagavad Gita in Its Own Time and Place,* this translation and commentary sets the Gita back into its rightful place as part of the Mahabharata and as a conversation on a battlefield between a warrior prince and a person who claimed and who proved Himself as the Supreme God.

Bhagavad Gita is a great gift to humanity. If possible, every human being should learn it and take from it the deep exposition about existence and our place in it.

Recommendation:

Alfredo Delregado submitted these comments regarding Chapters 2 and 3:

In the review of the most important verses from Chapter 2 that I wrote a few days ago, I summarized 3 parameters that made the commentaries in that chapter unique, as follows:

- *Buddhi yoga as Insight yoga.*
- *A Compliance Blueprint*
- *The independence of the author.*

These were the result of the interaction between Sankhya and buddhi yoga, the Yoga of the Intelligent Will. The emphasis in Chapter 2 is the withdrawal of the will from the most common human activities and desires; verily the Pratyahar of Patanjali. However good, this is not a complete yoga yet. Why? Because it does not include work, works, and the human being is always in action, conducting some work.

In Chapter 3, Krishna lectures Arjuna about the need for works, and how to work properly, and its relationship to the Supreme Person. This is trickle down ergonomics, for the Lord Himself cannot but to incessantly work, lest the world comes to a stop.

However, not surprisingly, the author's translation takes an unusual turn in translating the term karmanan in verse 3-4 as concerning "cultural activities" and not necessarily "works". Is there a difference? There is, and a substantial one. Why? Because of its interaction with social affairs. Here we have an author that emphasizes personal responsibilities greatly. And what is yoga, but that, finally? Likewise, in verse 3-5, the author again slides the meaning of karma and introduces "perform". This is a better fit for the verse, for indeed perform covers a broader spectrum than works, as one could be said to joyfully perform without working.

In this review of Chapter 3, my conclusions are similar, but when adapting them, they now read:

- Karma Yoga as the interaction of cultural activities within the frame of social affairs.
- Performance in that stage as the key to success, and morality as the gauge used for that success.
- The importance of the supernatural people.
- The independence of the author.

So far, the common thread is the independence of the author. It is a pity that more people are not privy of how this book came about.

Anu Gita Explained

Publisher: Michael Beloved

Date: September 30, 2011

ISBN:

Print: 9780983381792

eBook: 9780984001316

LCCN: 2011914434

Page Count: 310

Illustrations: 54

Size: 6" x 9" (inches)

Language: English

Category:

Body, Mind, Spirit, Reincarnation

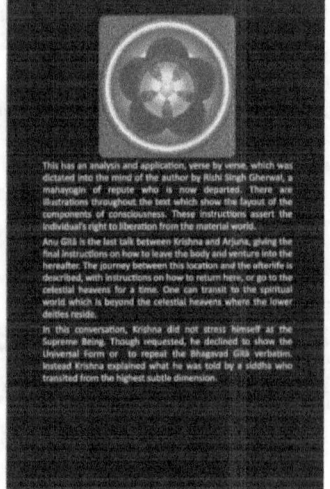

Back Cover:

This has an analysis and application verse by verse which was dictated into the mind of the author by Rishi Singh Gherwal, a mahayogin of repute who is now departed. There are illustrations throughout the text which show the layout of the components of consciousness. These instructions assert the individual's right to liberation from the material world.

Anu Gītā is the last talk between Krishna and Arjuna, giving the final instructions on how to leave the body and venture into the hereafter. The journey between this location and the afterlife is described, with instructions on how to return here, or go to the celestial heavens for a time.

One can go to the spiritual world which is beyond the celestial heavens where the lower deities reside. In this conversation, Krishna did not stress himself as the Supreme Being. Though requested, he declined to show the Universal Form or to repeat the Bhagavad Gita verbatim. Instead Krishna explained what he was told by a siddha who transited from the highest subtle dimension.

Description:

This is the translation with word-for-word meanings to the original Sanskrit. It has an analysis and application to all except the last three verses. No details are spared in the discussion about the transmigration journeys taken by a soul.

The journey through physical existence and hereafter and then back into this world, repeatedly, is neatly and precisely described by a siddha from a higher dimension. The soul, with the effect-energies from its socially-acceptable and criminal acts, travels to the hereafter where it is fittingly rewarded either in a heavenly world or a hellish place. Then it returns to this earthly planet and becomes adapted as an infant of parents.

Anu Gita is intense. It is Krishna's action thriller. Unlike the Bhagavad Gita where He explained many topics about the application of yoga proficiency to social involvement, the Anu Gita begins with an inquiry into the nature of the individual being and its transmigration between the physical world and the astral existence.

There is no drifting away from the topic. Krishna did not stress his divinity and supremacy as in the Bhagavad Gita. He simply quoted a discourse which occurred between a perfected siddha and Kashyapa.

Author's Comment:

This has an analysis and application verse by verse which was dictated into the mind of the author by Rishi Singh Gherwal, a mahayogin of repute who is now departed. There are illustrations throughout the text which show the layout of the components of consciousness. These instructions assert the individual's right to liberation from the material world.

Anu Gita is the last talk between Krishna and Arjuna, giving the final instructions on how to leave the body and venture into the hereafter. The journey between this location and the afterlife is described, with instructions on how to return here, or go to the celestial heavens for a time.

If qualified, one may go the spiritual world which is beyond the celestial heavens where the lower deities reside. Procedures for doing this are explained in the discourse. The boomerang effect of our earthly life is illustrated so vividly as to leave any reader with a clear idea of what can be done to alter the course of soul. It need not be restricted to that of taking one physical body after another in various mundane species of life.

Reviews:

-- John Wilson (Songtan, Korea):

Anu Gita Explained is much smaller than the other Gita Explained books by this author. And the writing seems to have evolved considerably. It took me three days to read all 270 pages and here's what I thought:

1. There were a lot more pictures than I expected.
2. The author clearly has a Ph.D. level understanding of our existence in this world and the preparation required to expertly TRANSIT OUT of it at the time of death.
3. The analysis and application of the ANCIENT AND ONCE-SECRET text is very clear. Imagine a sliding slope of evolutionary CONSCIOUSNESS and this writing explains how to move up or down on that evolutionary plane.
4. The MAIN POINTS that I took away from the book are:

- It is very important to MASTER ASTRAL PROJECTION before the end of this lifetime as that's the means of travel and operation after the spirit departs the flesh body.
- The CORE SPIRIT is made up of a spiritual quality and those who seek spirituality, seek to place the core self in a place that is on par with it 100%.
- Most individuals are focused on material existence, some individuals are focused religiously, and the least of individuals are focused on self-realization. This book is for all three but is of the most use to the latter category which has DETERMINATION.
- The author makes an excellent analogy...A slave (to material existence) who does not how he was captured can still PLAN HIS ESCAPE through observation and knowledge of his owner's habits.

Bottom line: If you are SEEKING, then this is the best book for you to read and it explains the ancient knowledge about eternal realities and machinations of the INNER PSYCHE. The last sentences of the book say, "This is all that is to be said. There is nothing beyond this. ......ONE WHO PRACTICES PROFICIENTLY AND CONSISTENTLY FOR SIX MONTHS ACCOMPLISHES THIS."

Kriya Yoga Bhagavad Gita

Publisher: Michael Beloved

Date: August 20, 2008

ISBN:

Print: 9780979391644

eBook: 9780983381754

LCCN: 2008906544

Page Count: 604

Illustrations: 2

Size: 7 x 10 x 1.4

Language: English

Category:

Body, Mind, Spirit, Meditation

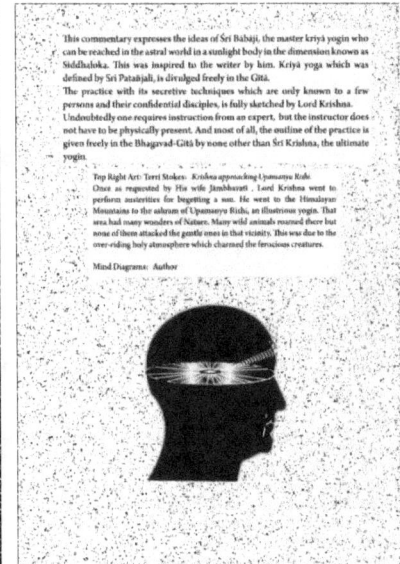

Back Cover:

This commentary expresses the ideas of Sri Babaji, the master kriya yogin who can be reached in the astral world in a sunlight body in the dimension known as Siddhaloka. This was inspired to the writer by him. Kriya yoga which was defined by Sri Patanjali, is divulged freely in the Gītā.

The practice with its secretive techniques which are only known to a few persons, and their confidential disciples, is fully sketched by Lord Krishna.

Undoubtedly one requires instruction from an expert, but the instructor does not have to be physically present. And most of all, the outline of the practice is given freely in the Bhagavad-Gītā by none other than Śrī Krishna, the ultimate yogin.

Description:

This precise and very revealing translation and commentary, exposes the kriya yoga techniques taught by Lord Krishna to Arjuna. This was inspired by Babaji Mahayogin, who uses a sunlight body and who imparted this information into the mind of the writer by mystic transfer.

Kriya yoga techniques are secretive but in contrast, Lord Krishna divulged it openly to Arjuna. This volume shows this. It may free a reader from ineffective kriya techniques. For practicing yogis, it would confirm valid kriyas and show new approaches.

Author's Comment:

Kriya yoga was always a mysterious yoga process, even in India. In this book I show the path of kriya yoga without secrecy. Most of all I uncover that it was shown to Arjuna by no other person than Lord Krishna, the foremost yogi. Both Lord Shiva and Lord Krishna are rated as supreme yogis.

Kriya yoga is not a difficult process but it does take a certain effort to turn away from extraneous cultural activities. It demands that one does so responsibly. You will not regret if you read through this commentary.

Reviews:

Too Precious!! -- by Beverly J. Cobb (Amazon customer review):

--- As it is, and how it should be. For elevating the psyche of those devotees/yogi's who are beyond religious dogma. A must have!! The content is priceless; it should be illegal.

Thank you, Yogi Madhvacarya!

Brahma Yoga Bhagavad Gita

Publisher: Michael Beloved

Date: December 9, 2008

ISBN:

Print: 9780979391651

ebook: 9780983381761

LCCN: 2008906545

Page Count: 538

Illustrations: 27

Size: 7 x 10 x 1.4 inches

Language: English

Category:

Body, Mind, Spirit, Spirituality

Back Cover:

Brahma yoga, regarded as the highest practice for meditation, is the method for keeping in touch with exclusive spiritual existence. There were a few great yogins who mastered this. One was Mahāsiddha Swami Nityānānda, the spiritual master of the reputed Siddha Swami Muktānānda.

Swami Nityānānda and Sri Bābāji Mahāśaya dictated most of these purports into the mind of the author. This commentary is specifically for those who practice brahma yoga. It is a useful introduction for anyone with a casual interest in its techniques.

Description:

This precise and very revealing translation and commentary, exposes the brahma yoga techniques hidden in the teachings Lord Krishna gave to Arjuna. This publication was inspired by Mahasiddha Swami Nityananda, who uses a causal body and who imparted this information into the mind of the writer by mystic transfer.

Brahma yoga techniques are secretive but in contrast, Lord Krishna divulged the process openly to Arjuna. This volume reveals this. It may free a reader from ineffective processes. For practicing yogis, it would confirm valid mystic methods and show new approaches to self-realization and the curbing of the human psyche.

Author's Comment:

Brahma Yoga is the most advanced meditation practice. It is not well known but Sri Krishna did touch on it in the Bhagavad Gita. If you read this it will give you some idea of how you can inch your way into the practice. This will greatly increase your admiration of Krishna.

Reviews:

Know your self through your Self -- by cpalacious (Amazon customer review):

This work is monumental! It is a revelation into the intricacies of the human psyche and into the mechanisms that keep all humans entrapped in this "mortal coil". Anyone interested in mastering their psychology should really look into this book. Furthermore, you should know that this is not the type of literature that is read once and then left in a bookshelf gathering dust. It is meant to be consulted time and time again as one advances on the spiritual path of yoga (or in any other spiritual path). The information found here is very humbling since one realizes that material existence is a colossus that has to be decapitated on a personal level. But once you realize what you are up against and decide to do something about it, divine grace will assist you along your way. So I suggest you get this book and start getting to know yourself through your Self!

Utterly Complete Masterpiece on Brahma Yoga -- by Dear Beloved:

Michael Beloved's rendering of this Bhagavad-Gita in the ultimate and most advanced context of Brahma Yoga is nothing short of amazing. The ancient science of Brahma Yoga is the highest practice in meditation and provides a definitive roadmap for reaching the spiritual existence. This commentary will give you an in-depth walk-through of all aspects of Brahma Yoga in relation to Krishna's teachings to Arjuna.

As I read this book, I continually wondered at the sheer psychological depth of the reading. The author's yogically-achieved grasp of human psychology is very evident.

Most of the book is written by Michael Beloved but clairvoyantly inspired by Swami Nityananda, an advanced yogi spirit who once inhabited this planet. I'll provide a few of the many key points for those who might be considering this book. In Brahma Yoga, one learns to develop dislike for both favorable and unfavorable circumstances. Pursuit of happiness is only beneficial if that happiness springs from one's indifference to material circumstances. Brahma Yoga Bhagavad Gita reveals how we can use this opportunity to "inquire into birth and death" as opposed to the normal pursuit of pleasure, expansion of vices, and development of science for the purpose of waging war and dominating others.

Furthermore, this book dissects the subtle organs of the body in the same manner as one would dissect a physical body. You will understand your inner workings, motivations, influences, energies, and more after reading this book. He traces the source of everything, not just on this physical level, but also on the invisible subtle and spiritual levels that can be accessed in varying manners according to your prevailing mode of depression, impulsion or clarity.

At one point he explains (through inspiration from Babaji Mahasaya) how the memory powers the intellect and thereby bothers student yogis. The key, he says, is to keep the intellect from supplying the memory with power to operate. Then one can achieve a blank state of mind and work to practice samadhi.

He banishes the idea of using idols and material objects for achieving success in the pursuit of liberation. These physical objects will not help one to gain mystic perception in the long run.

This 500+ page treatise on Brahma Yoga, on human, subtle and spiritual psychology, confirms the amazing completeness of the Bhagavad-Gita and lays the blueprint for any individual to master their inner psychology while escaping the whims of material nature. One's lack of knowledge and desire to perceive the truth should be one's main impetus to read this book and others like it. This will clear up your intellectual and mental darkness which is ever-present in the background and sometimes even in the forefront. So complete is this work that it's hard to find fault with anything, other than the occasional editing error.

Valuable Book -- by Nada (Amazon customer review):

A very interesting approach to the Bhagavad Gita.

A Book Well Worth the Reading -- by Neil W. Crenshaw (Amazon customer review):

This book should not be taken lightly by the serious practitioner of Brahma yoga or any other type of yoga as far as that goes. Brahma Yoga Bhagavad Gita is a detailed interpretation of the Bhagavad Gita as seen through the eyes of Yogi Madhvacarya (Michael Beloved) explained by The Master, Siddha Swami Nityananda.

The reader is taken through the Bhagavad Gita, step by step, with each verse interpreted with Brahma Yoga style transcription. The author explains in detail the meaning of Brahma yoga and how it relates to energy of the psyche.

What I like most about this book is the way the author translates the passages. Each and every passage of the Gita has the original Sanskrit writing followed by the pronunciation and the literal translation, word-for-word. This is an amazing feat in itself but the author goes on to add the English interpretation to that literal translation. Not only that but he also includes a commentary guided through him by his guru, Siddha Swami Nityananda. Although Nityananda died in 1961 Yogi Madhvacarya (Michael Beloved) received the psychic direction to write the commentary.

As far as I'm concerned, this is a very powerful book lending itself as a masterpiece in the world of yoga. As I read the verses I compared them to the Bhagavad-Gita as translated by Barbara Stoler Miller. Michael Beloved's and Miller's translation of the Gita, although somewhat different in composition, are refreshingly similar in interpretation. I also compared this book, Brahma Yoga Bhagavad Gita, to Michael Beloved's other book, Kriya Yoga Bhagavad Gita, and found that although the interpretations are the same the commentaries are quite different. This might seem contradictory on the surface but the differences compound the understanding of the conflict that was going on inside the warrior Arjuna.

Uddhava Gita Explained

Publisher: Michael Beloved

Date: April 8, 2009

ISBN:

Print: 9780981933214

Page Count: 740

Illustrations: 3

Size: 10 x 7 x 1.7 inches

Language: English

eBook: 9780983381778   **Category:**

LCCN: 2008911848   Body, Mind, Spirit

Back Cover:

Ever wondered if there are other dimensions? Ever conjectured that there must be more than this? Ever thought that the best spaceship would be your spirit or its subtle body? Ever found yourself in a dream in another interactive populated world?

In this discourse between Lord Krishna and Uddhava, features of many adjacent and remote parallel existences are detailed. The categories of the various spirits are discussed. The situation of the Supreme Being is described. The individual limited spirits are shown a passage to higher worlds. This is a deep-read. Take time.

Reveal it to yourself.

Description:

This translation and commentary is a deep-read, in-depth study of the instructions given to Uddhava who questioned Sri Krishna about the perplexities of material existence. In the teaching to Uddhava, Krishna stated that He taught three yogas, namely karma yoga, jnana yoga and bhakti yoga. In the Bhagavad Gita discussion with Arjuna, He admitted teaching only the first two of these. The complete teachings of Sri Krishna were given to Uddhava. All unanswered questions which Sri Krishna either avoided, or answered partially, are fully dealt with in the discourse with Uddhava. For that matter instead of advocating karma yoga which is detachment with worldly life, Sri Krishna insisted on jnana yoga, which is detachment and full abandonment of worldly life.

Karma yoga means that a person leaves aside the result of his or her activities, while jnana yoga means that a person refuses both the results and the opportunities for activity. And that was the path which Krishna recommended to Uddhava.

Author's Comment:

This book is a must for all persons who are interested in the Bhagavad Gita, and who suspected that what Lord Krishna explained to Arjuna was just part of the story. We were told by some Indian authorities, that the Bhagavad Gita's primary concern is bhakti yoga, but the text extols itself as being focused on karma yoga for making the warrior-prince Arjuna commit himself to duties on a war field.

Uddhava Gita is primarily concerned with jnana yoga and bhakti yoga combined. It discourages karma yoga. The value of this discourse with Uddhava is that it shows the alternative for those of us who are disinclined from karma yoga, from the approach laid out for Arjuna.

Apart from this, many secrets of the mystic lay-out of this existence are detailed to Uddhava. Much of this was not explained to Arjuna. As a practicing yogi, who travelled to other dimensions and saw the spiritual body of Sri Krishna, I assure you that after reading this, you will not have to read any other book about the subtle or spiritual existences.

This is the final explanation of spiritual reality.

Nobody can exceed this!

Reviews:

One of the Greatest Books on Yoga Ever Written -- by Alfredo Delregato

The author is a Yogi of the highest order, but not from India, the traditional land of yogis, but from Guyana and now settled in the United States. Yogi Madhvacharya Das has plumbed the depths of yoga. Perhaps there are few like him among us today. His yogic inclinations are deep-rooted and come from long and strenuous practices.

This book is a titanic endeavor. Only the Sanskrit elucidations place this work at a scholarly level with any other translations of Uddhava Gita. It is not an easy task to translate this ancient and many-meanings words language.

This is the last in a trilogy by the author regarding the three specific teachings of Lord Krishna. The first two, contained in the epic Mahabharata, were delivered to Arjuna; namely, the Bhagavad Gita and the Anu Gita. The last and most complete, was given later to Uddhava, and became known as the Uddhava Gita from the Srimad Bhagavatam.

It is perhaps important to emphasize the relevance to humankind of these three discourses. There is here esoteric knowledge of the highest order. But it is as important to highlight the specific purpose of the not well-known Uddhava Gita.

The book is masterfully structured, for it guides the reader first through the translations from Sanskrit to English for each verse which are designed for those interested in the meanings of the words and their intricacies. It follows with a very detailed commentary. It is here, in these commentaries, where the essence of this work is encountered and where deep attention is needed. It is in these provocative, esoteric dictums where the knowledge attained by intuition and deep yoga meditational practice is discerned. This is not a one-dimensional book, not even a two, or three-dimensional one, but a work of the highest spiritual order, a distillation of much wisdom that dabbles into the 4th dimensional spiritual realm.

The book contains 25 chapters. Each one is a jewel of yogic knowledge. Not only the Uddhava Gita is entertained, but there are many inroads, some of them in such depth so as to constitute by themselves short, compressed treatises, for example into the Yoga Sutras of Patanjali, as in Chapter 10 "Mystic Skills", or into Vedic Lore and the Manu Smritis, as in Chapter 12 "Righteous Lifestyle".

In summary, this is a yoga compendium of the highest quality and degree, and should be a primer for all aspiring and practicing yogis, as well as a book of reference for those interested in the esoteric teachings of Lord Krishna.

Yoga Sutras of Patanjali (paperback)

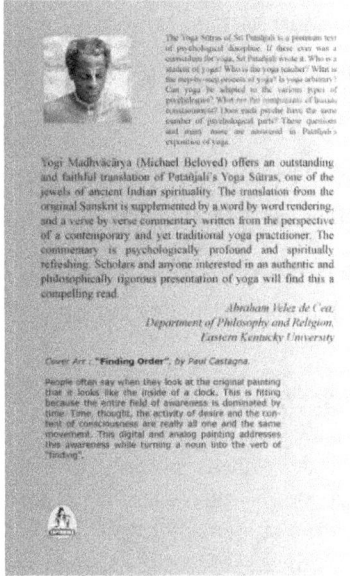

Yoga Sutras of Patanjali (hardbound)

A fresh translation and commentary from the original Sanskrit

Yogi Madhvāchārya / Michael Beloved

The Yoga Sūtras of Srī Patañjali is a premium text of psychological discipline. If there ever was a curriculum for yoga, Srī Patañjali wrote it. Who is a student of yoga? Who is the yoga teacher? What is the step-by-step process of yoga? Is yoga arbitrary? Can yoga be adapted to the various types of psychologies? What are the components of human consciousness? Does each psyche have the same number of psychological parts? These questions and many more are answered in Patañjali's exposition of yoga.

Yogi Madhvācārya (Michael Beloved) offers an outstanding and faithful translation of Patañjali's Yoga Sūtras, one of the jewels of ancient Indian spirituality. The translation from the original Sanskrit is supplemented by a word by word rendering, and a verse by verse commentary written from the perspective of a contemporary and yet traditional yoga practitioner. The commentary is psychologically profound and spiritually refreshing. Scholars and anyone interested in an authentic and philosophically rigorous presentation of yoga will find this a compelling read.

Abraham Velez de Cea
Department of Philosophy
and Religion,
Eastern Kentucky University

Cover Art : "The Wheel", by Paul Castagna.
People often say when they look at the original painting that it looks like the inside of a clock. This is fitting because the entire field of awareness is dominated by time. Time, thought, the activity of desire and the content of consciousness are really all one and the same movement. This digital and analog painting addresses this awareness while turning a noun into the verb of "finding".

$28.95 US

Publisher: Michael Beloved

ISBN:

eBook: pending

paperback: 9780979391613

hardbound: 9780979391668

paperback LCCN: 2010918321

hardbound LCCN: 2008906317

Date: April 28, 2008

Page Count: 244

Illustrations: 2

Size: 8.8 x 6 x 0.7 inches

Language: English

Category:

Religion and Spirituality

Back cover:

The Yoga Sūtras of Śrī Patañjali is a premium text of psychological discipline. If there ever was a curriculum for yoga, Śrī Patañjali wrote it. Who is a student of yoga? Who is the yoga teacher? What is the step-by-step process of yoga? Is yoga arbitrary? Can yoga be adapted to the various types of psychologies? What are the components of human consciousness? Does each psyche have the same number of psychological parts? These questions and many more are answered in Patañjali's exposition of yoga.

Cover Art: "Finding Order", by Paul Castagna.

People often say when they look at the original painting that it looks like the inside of a clock. This is fitting because the entire field of awareness is dominated by time. Time, thought, the activity of desire and the content of consciousness are really all one and the same movement. This digital and analog painting addresses this awareness while turning a noun into the verb of "finding".

Description:

--- A fresh translation of Yoga Sutras of Patanjali, with word-for-word meanings and precise commentary. --- New insight into the advanced practices of meditation, kriya yoga and raja yoga. - A gift from a great yogin.

Author's Comment:

I recommend a detailed study of Sri Patanjali Maharshi's Yoga Sutras. His lay-out is the curriculum for yoga. It is classic and final. Nobody can improve it. At first reading this book might seem difficult but if you are patient, you will get much insight about Yoga.

Reviews:

-- By Abraham Velez de Cea, Department of Philosophy and Religion, Eastern Kentucky University:

Yogi Madhvacharya (Michael Beloved) offers an outstanding and faithful translation of Patañjali's Yoga Sutras, one of the jewels of ancient Indian spirituality. The translation from the original Sanskrit is supplemented by a word by word rendering, and a verse by verse commentary written from the perspective of a contemporary and yet traditional yoga practitioner. The commentary is psychologically profound and spiritually refreshing. Scholars and anyone interested in an authentic and philosophically rigorous presentation of yoga will find this a compelling read.

-- By Marcia Metusalem:

Serious students of yoga and meditation will find this book intellectually and spiritually stimulating. The translation stays true to the Sanskrit and is terse, leaving little room for speculation. Part 2, the "approach" to the

Sutras, gives needed relief to readers who might grasp the translation but nevertheless have difficulty integrating Patanjali's in depth analysis of the yoga process. Some readers may find it easier to begin at Part 2 and then go on to Parts 1 and 3.The commentaries contain useful information and explanations relating to the Sutras and also give a unique perspective based on the writer's own yoga practice. A persistent reader will not be disappointed for between the lines one finds the faith, inspiration and encouragement to try for success in yoga.

-- By Neil Crenshaw (Amazon customer review):

This is the best book that I've been able to find on the Yoga Sutras and I have reviewed several on the subject. The Yoga Sutras of Patanjali by Michael Beloved is very easy and enjoyable to read. Michael Beloved divides his book into three parts: 1) the Sanskrit text of Patanjali with Michael's translation, 2) a brief explanation of what each verse means, in English and 3) a simple translation and commentary on each chapter and verse.

The third part of the book is where I spent most of my time. This part has Patanjali's actual Sanskrit words with Michael's translation of those words and then Michael's commentary about Patanjali's work and meaning for that particular topic. The commentary gave me a better understanding of what Patanjali was trying to convey. The three parts can be read separately or at the same time. I preferred reading the three parts, together. I put a paper clip on the first page of each chapter and flipped back-and-forth from one part to the other, reading one verse at a time as I went along. This gave me greater understanding, insight and appreciation for Patanjali's work. This book is a work of art. I highly recommend this book to anyone interested in yoga, ancient texts of the eastern world or spirituality.

Index

About Michael Beloved

Michael Beloved took his current body in 1951 in Guyana. In 1965, while living in Trinidad, he instinctively began doing yoga postures and trying to make sense of the supernatural side of life. Later on, in 1970, in the Philippines, Michael approached a Martial Arts Master named Mr. Arthur Beverford. He explained that he wanted a yoga instructor. Beverford identified himself as a disciple of the great yogin, Rishi Singh Gherwal. Beverford taught him the traditional Ashtanga Yoga with stress on postures, attentive breathing and brow chakra centering meditation. In 1972, he entered the Denver Colorado Ashram of Kundalini Yoga and took instruction in Bhastrika Pranayama and its application to yoga postures. Later in 1979, he formally entered the spiritual society founded by Bhaktivedanta Prabhupada.

Michael no longer participates in any formal spiritual groups or societies; however in recent years, he devoted much time to writing multiple interpretations of the Bhagavad Gita including a focus on kriya yoga, karma yoga, and brahma yoga. He also translated the Uddhava Gita and provided a detailed commentary of the masterpiece. Most of his work is deeply philosophical and psychological in nature and is a reflection of a lifetime of dedication and austerity towards passing on the knowledge of those who instructed him.

Michael's specialty is kundalini yoga and advanced meditation which was explained by Patanjali Mahayogin, as samyama which is the sequential development of linking one's attention to a higher reality, first with special effort, then spontaneously, and finally without effort and continuously.

Order Form

BOOK	Price	Quantity	Total
Anu Gita English	$7.99		
Anu Gita Explained	$13.99		
Astral Projection	$8.95		
Bhagavad Gita English	$9.99		
Bhagavad Gita Explained	$24.99		
Bhagavad Gita Revealed	$12.99		
Brahma Yoga Bhagavad Gita	$22.95		
Krishna Cosmic Body	$13.99		
Kriya Yoga Bhagavad Gita	$24.95		
Markandeya Samasya English	$7.99		
Meditation Expertise	$13.99		
Meditation Pictorial	$13.99		
sex you!	$11.99		
Sleep Paralysis	$7.95		
Spiritual Master	$11.99		
Uddhava Gita English	$11.99		
Uddhava Gita Explained	$28.99		
Yoga Sutras English	$7.99		
Yoga Sutras of Patanjali (paperback)	$13.99		
Yoga Sutras of Patanjali (hardbound)			
Sub-total:			
SHIPPING & Handling: $3.99 for 1st book plus $1 for each single copy of an additional book. Please contact us for bulk purchases.			
TOTAL:			

Name:

Shipping Address:

Street:--

City: --

State: --

Zip Code: ------------------------------------

Country: --

Phone: --

Email: --

Please allow 2-3 weeks for delivery.

Contact, Inquiries

Bulk Orders: michaelbelovedbooks@gmail.com

Phone	**937-305-0717.**
	347-768-5341
Please render a check or money order to:	**Michael Beloved**
	18311 NW 8th Street
	Pembroke Pines
	FL **33029**
	USA

Books may also be ordered **online** through **Amazon, Kindle, Nook and Kobo.** When ordering online, use a link in this publication or conduct a search by **ISBN, Title or Author**.

Write Us --- Visit Our Website and Forum

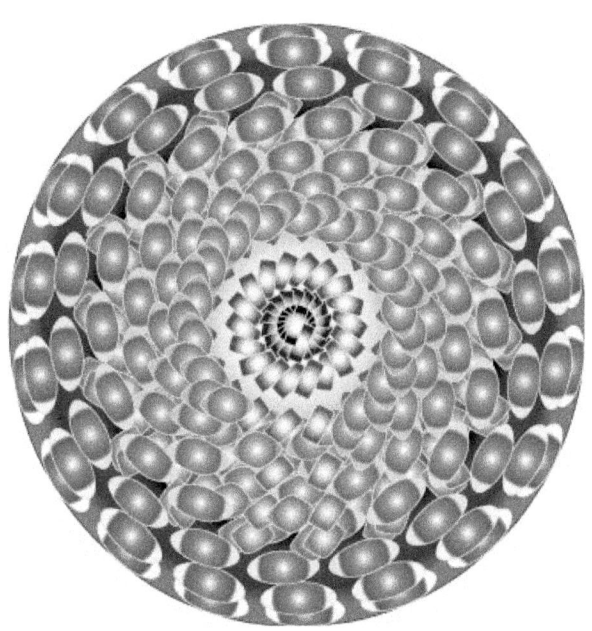

Email:	michaelbelovedbooks@gmail.com
	axisnexus@gmail.com
Website:	michaelbeloved.com
	https://sites.google.com/site/michaelbeloved/
Forum:	inselfyoga.com
	http://meditationtime.grou.ps/